20p

STARSTORMERS

'*The Worst Thing on Earth is here and now: being a boarder at this school. Being left behind as a prisoner. Knowing your parents are a thousand million miles away.*'

Worst Thing on Earth is just a game, a way of passing time, until Vawn, Makenzi and Ispex are pushed into action by Tsu.

Together they ransack junkyards, seeking out the necessary components for their spaceship – a hollowed-out meteorite.

When it's finished the game takes a more serious, nerve-racking turn. Mak's finger is poised on the button, ready to blast Starstormer and her crew – to what . . . ?

This is the first story in the Starstormer Saga

SUNBURST, the second part of the Starstormer Saga, is also published by Knight Books.

Knight Books also publish

FLAMERS by Nicholas Fisk
(First published in hardback under the title ESCAPE FROM SPLATTERBANG)

Other science fiction novels by Nicholas Fisk include:

SPACE HOSTAGES
TRILLIONS
HIGH WAY HOME
LITTLE GREEN SPACEMAN
WHEELIE IN THE STARS
TIME TRAP
MONSTER MAKER
GRINNY
ANTIGRAV
A RAG, A BONE AND A HANK
OF HAIR

Starstormers

Nicholas Fisk

KNIGHT BOOKS
Hodder and Stoughton

First published by Knight Books 1980

British Library C.I.P.

Fisk, Nicholas
Starstormers.
I. Title
823' .9'1 J PZ7.F548

ISBN 0-340-24878-5

The characters and situations in this book are entirely imaginary and bear no relation to any real person or actual happening

Printed and bound in Great Britain for Hodder and Stoughton Paperbacks, a division of Hodder and Stoughton Ltd., Mill Road, Dunton Green, Sevenoaks, Kent (Editorial Office: 47 Bedford Square, London, WC1 3DP) by Hunt Barnard Printing, Ltd, Aylesbury, Bucks.

THE ROARING SKY

Every few minutes, sometimes several times in one minute, you heard the roaring in the sky.

Most often, the vast sounds just came from nowhere, instantly, and hit you – SMASH!, like that. In the old days, the twentieth century days, at least you had warning. The roarings announced themselves, so to speak. There would be a distant, warning sound, then the full sound, then the dying sound as the jetliner went on its way.

There were still people alive who remembered those sounds and those days. 'Oh, it was dreadful, our house was near the airport, right under the flight path, you see, and all day long it was noise, noise, noise from the jets, you couldn't sit in your own garden . . . ' So your grandfather or grandmother might tell you. You would nod politely, thinking, 'It's a good thing the poor old dear is so deaf.'

But even as you thought this – BLAM!, and yet another ship howled or bellowed or thunderclapped its way out of Earth's atmosphere, making a noise like a mad pop group in a thunderstorm or a smash-up or the end of the world, depending on whether it was a freighter, an Interstar or a military ship.

'Oh yes, it was dreadfully noisy in the twentieth century,' grandmother or grandfather would tell you; you'd murmur, 'Hmm'. But even before you'd finished your 'Hmm', there would be another catastrophic BLAM! as another ship left Earth and your heart skipped another beat. The ships were so big, so vast, so fast. Faster than sound. The noise reached you after the ship made it. That was why there was never any warning.

The noise was perhaps the worst thing about Earth in the twenty-first century. No, wait: not the worst, not the worst by any means . . .

SCHOOL

'Let's play Worst Thing on Earth,' Vawn said, resting her bare feet on Ispex's back. Her own back was jammed against the dried-out, cracking panelled wall of the common room, still showing the initials carved two centuries ago. She was bent almost double so that her mane of coppery brown hair completely hid her face. She was twelve.

'The Worst Thing on Earth,' she began, 'is here and now: being a boarder in this school. Being left behind as a prisoner. Knowing your parents are a thousand million miles away. Knowing you can't escape. Your turn, Ispex.'

'The Worst Thing on Earth,' little Ispex said, glinting his spectacles earnestly at the other two, 'is crumminess. Knowing you're stuck with a loser. Knowing that the whole planet is going down and down, everything falling apart, nothing working, everyone wanting to leave, all the best people already gone – '

'Everyone but us,' Makenzi said. He was the tallest of the three and at fourteen, the oldest. He scratched his crinkled black hair with a long finger, dark brown one side, pale brown the other. His forebears were West Indian. His grandparents had settled in Scotland, long ago, in the twentieth century, building the tankers that carried oil when there was still oil. 'Everyone but us,' he repeated gloomily, looking like a caged cat, a black puma, in the battered, dismal old room.

He stretched his arms above his head, jumped, and caught hold of a beam. He began to do pull-ups, grunting with effort. 'The Worst Thing on Earth,' he said, 'is us. US!'

He dropped from the beam and loomed over Ispex. 'Why are we here?' he bellowed in Ispex's face. 'Why don't our parents come and get us? Why don't we just get *out*, go *away*?'

Ispex stared back at him, mildly.

'And why do you wear those crazy spectacles?' Makenzi demanded. 'Are you a freak, or something? An antique?' Now Makenzi was grinning. He had deliberately changed his mood, trying to throw off the grey cloud that was always over them, the cloud that would brood above them as long as they remained on Earth, away from the real worlds, the worlds that glittered and beckoned in the night sky.

Ispex said, with dignity, 'I prefer spectacles. My eyes cannot tolerate contact lenses. It is a medical condition. I *like* my glasses.' He took them off, bent his round sandy head over them and polished them with his special cloth.

Vawn kicked out at his back, jogging him, but he took no notice. 'You're really an old man in disguise, you know that?' she said. There was still a trace of Irish in her voice. In the old days, her name would have been Siobhan, 'Shevawn'. 'You're an animated fossil,' she said, lazily.

Ispex polished his glasses. 'You've said that before,' he said. Then, severely, 'We should *think*.'

'Think what?' Makenzi said.

Vawn uncoiled herself and looked round the common room, blinking her pale grey eyes, making her long face even longer with a yawn. She vaguely noted the rain splashing the windows, the battered locker doors ringing the gingery-brown room, the sagging plastic chairs, the school notices all askew and curling on the notice board by the door. She yawned again, noisily.

'That's not thinking,' Ispex said to her, severely. 'That's yawning. To think constructively, you must establish the facts and put them in a proper order. Then you can arrive at an effective conclusion.'

They had ignored or even not noticed the fourth person in the room: a figure almost hidden in a window recess. 'I quite agree,' Tsu said, in her high, clipped, precise voice. 'It's no good just sitting here – '

'Nobody asked *you*,' Makenzi said, with deliberate rudeness. 'Come to that, nobody asked *you* to join us. Even sit with us. You don't belong.'

'I do belong. I belong because I want to get out. I want to leave Earth, like you – '

'We've got somewhere to go. We've got parents waiting for us,' Makenzi said. 'You haven't any parents. So you don't belong.'

Vawn, shocked, 'Mak! There's no need to – '

Makenzi cut across her. 'All right, all right,' he said. 'I'm cruel and nasty to poor little Tsu. But I don't care. What I said is true. I'm *serious*, I really do want to get out. We really do intend to get to our parents on Epsilon Cool. The three of us – me,

Ispex and you, Vawn – will do it somehow. But we don't want any passengers. We can't carry anyone. Particularly not Junior School kids like Tsu.'

Tsu stood up. She was a foot shorter than Makenzi and three years younger. Her skin was golden yellow. Her black hair, so dark that it seemed to have blue lights in it, swept back in two wings, clipped short. The irises of her eyes seemed almost black under the heavy curved eyelids. Her small, delicately boned hands were at rest. She said, 'I'll fight you.'

Makenzi laughed aloud. 'You won't,' he said. 'You most certainly won't! *You* fight *me*?'

'I'll fight you. I'll beat you. Then you'll let me come. I'm not a passenger, a hanger-on. I'll prove it. I'll fight you.'

Makenzi deliberately stared into Tsu's eyes. 'No fight, no way,' he said.

'You're yellow,' Tsu said.

Makenzi grinned and said, 'That's good, coming from a Chinese!' As he said the words, he flinched and dropped his eyes. Vawn said, 'Mak! How could you!' Ispex stared at Makenzi and said, 'Apologise. Say you're sorry.'

Tsu said, 'I don't want apologies. I want to fight. With *you*.'

Makenzi mumbled, 'I'm sorry. I apologise. I didn't mean – '

'Never mind that. I like to be Chinese, that is why my name is Tsu, T-S-U, instead of Sue. It is not my fault that the Chinese rule the world and rule it badly. The world was bad when the whites ruled it. Will you fight me?'

'No, I told you – '

'But I must prove to you – '

'No.'

Without a word, Tsu turned and left. She looked very small and neat as she crossed the dingy room. When she was gone, Vawn said, 'You're a pig, Makenzi.'

'I know. But I didn't mean it, it all builds up . . . You know what I mean, all the Chinese jokes . . . Everyone jealous of them . . . I just didn't think.'

'It's time we thought,' Ispex said. 'Let's think properly. I'll begin. First why are we here? Because – '

'Because it's the dumping ground of the galaxy, and we're dumped,' Vawn said, bitterly. ' "The Left-behind Children".' Makenzi seemed not to be listening. He was picking at a tuft of thread on the worn-out floor covering.

'All right,' Ispex said. 'How long will we stay dumped?'

'Until our parents finish the settlement on Epsilon Cool and pick us up and take us *home* . . . A home with *them* . . . ' She hugged her knees.

'All right. And when will that be?'

'Never,' said Makenzi, suddenly rejoining the other two. 'We're dumped for life the way things are going.'

'Not necessarily so,' Ispex said, primly. 'Epsilon Cool *should* have been made habitable by now; the settlements and life-support systems and agriculture *should* have been completed – '

'But they're not,' said Makenzi. 'And my bet is

that they won't be for years. Listen, Ispex – if you were going to say, "Oh, let's be patient, let's play cool, it can't be much longer" – if that's what you think, I *don't*. No new world for us. We're stuck with what's left of the old one. Stuck indefinitely.' He began to sing, mockingly, 'Why are we waiting.'

Overhead, there was a thunder clap that shook the school. 'Starship,' Makenzi said. 'Outward bound, of course . . . ' He stared through the window at the sky but there was nothing to see. 'We've got to *do* something,' he said. 'Do it *now*. Get *out*.'

'All right, we're agreed. We won't wait. We'll get out,' said Ispex. 'But how? We've discussed various plans. Let's go through them all over again and this time really think about them. First, stowaways.'

'Stowing away never works,' Vawn said. 'I mean, look at last night's TV! All those people trying to get out . . . children, too. The police and Emigration Control were packing them away in vanloads – '

'*Some* stowaways *must* make it,' Makenzi objected, 'and those would be the ones you *don't* learn about.'

'If they do make it, they get caught at the other end and sent back,' Ispex said, silencing Makenzi by holding up a schoolmasterly forefinger. 'Tsu would be. She's an orphan. No parents to accept her. That's why we particularly don't want her homing in on us. Now, do we or don't we vote to try stowing away?'

A bellowing, slamming roar from the sky silenced him. When it was over, Makenzi said, 'That shuttle that just went over – I'd take my chance on a ship like that.'

Ispex said, 'Would *you*, Vawn?'

She thought, her hair hiding her face; then looked up and said, 'No. I vote no. They'd get us.'

'I vote no, too,' said Ispex. 'Well . . . at least we've *thought* about it . . . '

Ispex went on, trying to make his voice decisive and firm, 'Plan two: Certificate of Special Urgency, issued on compassionate grounds – '

'Oh, that,' Makenzi said. 'They don't swallow that stuff any more, it's no good trying that on – '

'In the old days,' Ispex said, 'people made themselves ill by chewing soap. You get a temperature and everything. I read it in an old book – '

'You and your old books!'

'Well, it might be worth a try. We make ourselves ill, and the Certificate is issued and our parents are given leave to come and collect us – '

'This is the twenty-first century,' Makenzi said, wearily. 'Present-day doctors *know* about *soap*.'

Ispex said, 'But it's an old dodge, they might not – '

'Look,' Makenzi interrupted, 'why don't we do something useful? Why don't we set fire to the dormitories, or hit each other on the head with heavy objects, or dress up as bunny rabbits and chew grass, or build a spaceship – '

'Build a spaceship,' said Vawn, looking up. 'Did you say, *build a spaceship?*'

'*Build a spaceship?*' said Ispex. His mouth opened

into an O. His spectacles glittered in the grey light. 'You said, *build* a spaceship?'

Makenzi stared from one face to another. 'Look,' he said, 'I was only talking, it was only words, I wasn't serious – '

But Vawn and Ispex were still staring at him, or at nothing. 'Build one . . . !' Ispex muttered.

Makenzi uttered a strangled '!' and said, 'Mad, you're going mad, *I'm* going mad! For heaven's sake, come on, let's go and find some food or something! Are you coming?' Neither replied.

Makenzi snorted and left, slamming the door.

Waiting outside the door was Tsu.

'Will you fight me?' she said to Makenzi, in her thin, cool voice.

'What the – ! I told you, *no* – '

'Then I'll fight you,' she replied, and hit him in the neck with the edge of her hand.

Makenzi discovered that he was lying on the dirty floor of the corridor, one side of his neck a solid agony.

THE FIGHT

Vawn and Ispex heard Makenzi fall and came running.

Makenzi was still sprawled on the floor. He got slowly to his feet, rubbing his neck. 'Well,' he said, 'thank you, thank you very much . . . ' He shook his head. His eyes were furious.

'Fight,' said Tsu.

'I told you: no. I don't fight little girls. Go away.'

'Fight,' she said, and kicked him. The kick came from nowhere. It was like a dance movement, controlled and dainty. The kick again hit Makenzi in the throat. He staggered back choking, his eyes rolling and glowing darkly with fury.

Tsu said, 'Here or in the gym. But you'd better fight.'

He was so angry that he lashed out at her with a big, swinging open-handed slap aimed at her face. She swayed backwards a very little – and again her foot came up. This time it caught him in the solar plexus.

He gasped, stared at her calm face in amazement and went for her with his right fist clenched. Vawn shouted, 'Stop!' and pulled at his shoulder. Tsu kicked yet again and Makenzi shouted with pain and surprise. He flung Vawn aside, opened his shoulders and let fly a punch at Tsu.

Quick as she was, it landed solidly on the top

of her arm, at the shoulder. For the first time, her face showed some emotion. Small white teeth were revealed as her lips parted. For a second, her heavily lidded eyes opened wide. She swayed sideways with the shock of the punch, yet in the same movement somehow half turned, swivelled and hit out back-handed with a chopping blow. It struck Makenzi's throat with a vicious slapping sound.

But his muscles were hard with fury: he seemed not to notice the blow. He moved in on her, arms outstretched. He had his left hand round Tsu's throat and his right raised, his big fist ready to hit her.

He could not bring himself to strike. Then Ispex was clumsily pulling at him, clumsily wrapping his arms round Makenzi's waist and hooting, 'Be reasonable, be reasonable', as if he were a preacher in a village church. Still Makenzi could not strike. Still Tsu's face was unmoved, although Makenzi's hand was clenched on her throat.

She did something to his wrist, something strange and quick and mysterious, and Makenzi spun away from her, feet off the ground, a blur of whirling legs and wide-open mouth and a big hand clawing at nothing as he flew through the air. His feet slammed down on the floor.

But he had her hand. He pulled and twisted at it as he fell. Suddenly she was on the floor too and Makenzi had hopped sideways like a great insect. He was astride her, with both her small hands locked in his big ones and his knees crushing down her shoulders.

She gasped and winced and kicked at his back. The kicks slapped without power. He said, 'Please! Enough!' as if he were the one pinned down. She only kicked more furiously.

'Please! Let's stop!'

Now there were tears in her eyes, tears of pain and rage. But still she writhed and kicked.

'I'm twice your weight! . . . Please!' Makenzi pleaded, but now she was trying to get a knee into his armpit so that she could lever him off. Her mouth was twisted. Her teeth showed.

'You win!' Makenzi shouted. 'Do you understand? I give in! *You win!*'

As if the words were magic, she instantly went limp. Her face became calm. 'I win,' she said. 'You admit it?'

'Win, admit, anything you like,' he said. 'It's all ridiculous – '

'So I can come with you?'

'Come where? What do you mean? I didn't say – '

'You must let me come with you. Wherever you are going. If you don't, I'll fight you again. Again and again.'

Makenzi whistled faintly and looked up at Vawn and Ispex. Vawn nodded her head: Ispex said, 'She means it,' and shrugged.

Slowly and cautiously, Makenzi disentangled himself from Tsu. He stood and helped her up. The yellow-gold of her face was another paler colour and she was trembling. She said, 'You agree, then? I'm one of you now?'

Makenzi gently put his hands on her shoulders

and squeezed them enquiringly.

'Are you all right? Does this hurt?'

'Of course not. I won. So I'm coming with you,' she said.

'Coming where? Tell us where we're going, we don't know!'

'On the starship you're going to make. I listened through the keyhole.'

'You're joking!'

'Were *you* joking?'

'Well, we certainly weren't serious. Tell her, Ispex.'

Ispex said, 'We were only talking. You can't make starships. It stands to reason – '

'We'll make a starship,' Tsu said. 'We can, I know we can. We'll go to Epsilon Cool. The four of us. Now I am going to have a shower.'

They watched her in amazement as she walked away. 'She's so *small*!' Vawn said, wonderingly.

'That's why I couldn't hit her,' Makenzi said, ruefully rubbing his throat. 'She doesn't fight small,' he added. 'She's a bomb, a dragon. She certainly hit *me*. Wow.'

'Wow,' said Vawn.

Somewhere a bell rang, and there was the distant echoing noise of shouts and running footsteps. Doors burst open, flying figures thundered past. Fourth-formers. One of them stopped. 'Heh! Where were you? Mr Whiting came round, he said he's taken your names, you're going to catch it this time!'

'Boo hoo,' said Makenzi. 'I'm so frightened. Run along.' He put his foot against the seat of the fourth-former's denims and pushed.

'We've got to talk,' Ispex said.

'More talk?' said Vawn.

'Spacecraft,' said Ispex, stolidly. 'Starship. How to build one.'

'But you *can't* build – '

'Let's *think*,' said Ispex and led them back into the common room. '*Really* think,' he said, and closed the door carefully behind him.

THE METEORITE

They thought and nothing happened.

They thought again and Vawn's head drooped until her face was completely curtained by her hair. Yawns and groans were faintly heard from behind the curtains. She was working herself into one of her Big Glooms, her silent depressions. They could last for days. Makenzi pretended to be asleep. Only Ispex kept on.

'If we stole the components,' he said, 'we could at least get some sort of drive unit together – a magnetic scoop, something like that. Why aren't you two listening?'

Vawn moaned. Makenzi said, 'Oh, shut *up*. You know what, Vawn? I think I'll start wearing a kilt. After all, I'm a Scot, aren't I? Och aye, the noo, a wee Scottish laddie.' He began imitating bagpipes, stopped, and said to Ispex, 'Look there's no way we can beg, borrow, steal, hijack or make a spaceship – '

'There must be a way if only we *think*,' said Ispex solemnly. 'I mean, if we got the drive unit–'

The door opened and Tsu came in. 'Well?' she said.

'Well what?'

'Well, what are you going to do?'

'Watch TV,' said Makenzi. 'That's what I'm going to do.' He prodded a switch. At once the telly wall was ablaze with coloured images, often in 3D – particularly the commercials. Giant mothers fed enormous babies with monster helpings of sloppy foods. Tsu said, 'Must we have this on?' and moved to switch the wall off.

Ispex said, 'No! Wait!' and stared at the wall. The news had started.

Tsu said, 'But we've got to make plans – '

'Quiet! Watch!'

They watched the news programme. The voice from the wall said, ' . . . these giant specimens were collected by an Interstellar ship commanded by Captain Chan Sing. Tell me, Captain, is there anything of unusual interest about these meteorites you've brought back to Earth?'

'Meteorites again!' said Makenzi scornfully. 'Who cares about meteorites?'

'Watch!' Ispex insisted. Unwillingly, they obeyed. The Chinese captain of the Interstellar talked and talked, using technical terms that only Ispex understood. The captain grinned, made gestures, explained: the cameras closed in on him or the meteorites, great chunks of rocky rubbish, big as houses, scooped up in space –

Vawn protested. 'Switch off! Let's go and eat, or something!' Ispex did not even hear her. He was hunched forward, staring at the screen, biting his lower lip. The coloured images made dancing reflections on his glasses.

'And now – sport!' said the TV voice.

Ispex let out the breath he had bottled up. 'That could be it!' he whispered. 'That could be the answer!'

'What answer? What question?' Makenzi demanded.

'A meteorite!' said Ispex. 'Don't you see? Surely you see!'

'Explain,' said Tsu.

'Well, it's obvious! You've only got to think! Where do meteorites come from?'

'Space,' said Vawn, in a bored voice. 'Look, I'm hungry – '

'That's it! Space! So that tells you one important thing about meteorites!' said Ispex.

'What important thing? Is anyone else hungry?' Vawn said. But Tsu said, 'Go on!'

'It tells you,' Ispex said, impressively, 'that meteorites are spaceworthy! Now do you see!'

Makenzi said, 'No. Explain.' Now he was curious.

'But it's simple! There we were, talking about hulls, and metals, and all the complications of making a spacecraft, when all the time the answer was there – *meteorites*! A meteorite is your spacecraft hull! Ready-made! Flight-tested! Spaceworthy!'

Vawn said, 'So we're to sit astride a meteorite and ride it to Epsilon Cool!'

Ispex waved her to silence. 'You begin with a meteorite,' he said. 'Any meteorite big enough to hold people and the things they need – their ecosuits, fuel, food and all the rest of it. Then you get hold of a laser team somehow – and you make them hollow out the meteorite. They cut away and make – '

'Living quarters, fuel stores, drive mountings!'

Makenzi shouted. 'Hollow everything out until you've got a spaceship!'

'A spaceship!' said Tsu. 'A starship!'

'First catch your meteorite,' Vawn said, trying to hide her excitement.

'That's easy,' Tsu said. 'I've got money. And they're always bringing back meteorites; like that Interstellar Captain we saw just now. They scoop them up, bring them back, hope there's something unusual or valuable – '

'Then find there *isn't*!' Ispex continued for her. 'So then what do they do?'

'Dump them,' said Makenzi. 'Dump them in dumps, dumpity dump. Because they're useless rubbish – not valuable after all.'

'And there's at least one dump near here,' said Tsu.

The TV painted the four of them with the colours from its giant images. Unheeded, it told things or sold things. None of the four watched. Their heads were close together, their eyes alight with something brighter than anything the TV could show, something more startling than any of the slamming explosions that filled the grey skies outside . . .

'And now, we've got to *think*,' said Ispex, yet again, as he drew the very first sketches and lettered them in with untidy, wobbling handwriting.

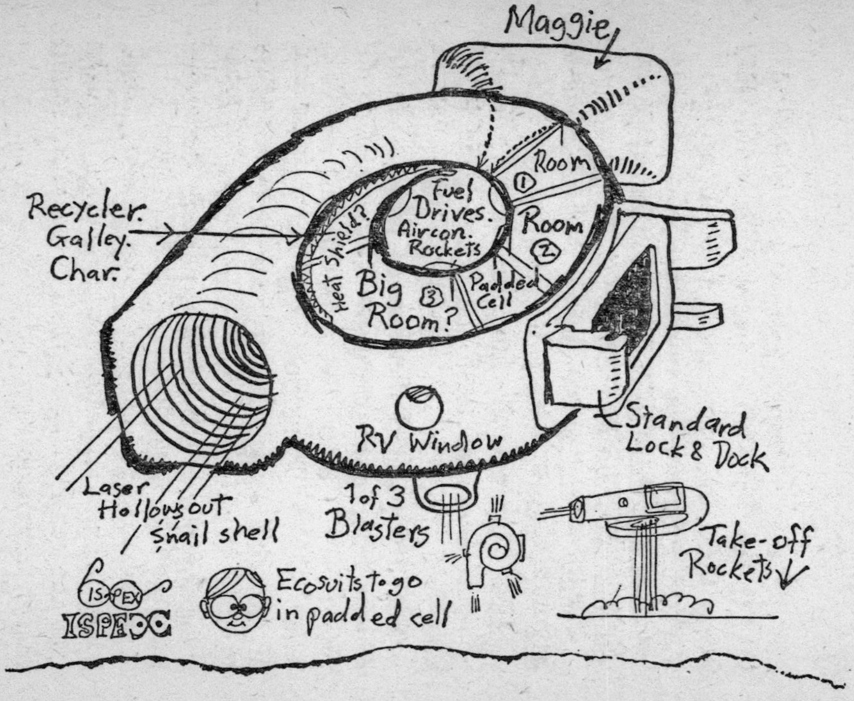
Maggie
Room ①
Room ②
Fuel
Drives.
Aircon.
Rockets
Padded Cell
Big ③ Room?
Heat Shields?
Recycler.
Galley.
Char.
RV Window
Standard
Lock & Dock
Laser
Hollows out
snail shell
1 of 3
Blasters
Take-off
Rockets
IS PEX
ISPEDC
Ecosuits to go
in padded cell

THE HULL

For being absent from class, Mr Whiting gave them three days detention. He didn't care: they didn't care.

Outside the tumbledown old boarding school, the rain beat down, finding its way through the slipping tiles on the rotting roofs.

The three of them met in the attics, hidden and forgotten, and made plans.

'Tsu,' Makenzi said. 'She still worries me.' He lay on his back with his mouth open, letting drops of leaking rainwater fall straight into his mouth. 'We've got to find a way of freezing her out. I mean, we three have always been together, we understand each other – '

'She's the only one who's doing anything useful at this moment,' Ispex said. 'There you are, lying on your back, and she's down at the junk-yards, sussing out meteorites. And anyhow, she really does have money. We'll need money.'

'She'll be getting rather wet,' Vawn said, contentedly. Her rainwater leaks fell straight into the self-heating Glocan. Soon there would be hot water and then coffee.

'She won't get anywhere, wet or dry,' Makenzi said. 'They're a hard lot, those junkers.'

'There used to be rag-and-bone men,' Ispex remarked. 'I've read about them.'

'In an old book?' Makenzi said.

'Yes – '

'You and your old books . . . '

A freighter took off from somewhere. BLAM! The shock shifted another decaying tile another thousandth of an inch. The rain beat down harder. The leak above Makenzi became a minor downpour. He closed his mouth and moved his head.

'Poor Tsu,' he said, and grinned.

THE JUNKYARD

As usual in junkyards and other such places, the boss was 'out'.

But the owner was there: a paunchy middle-aged man wearing an expensive wig and a real leather cap on top of it. 'Rich,' thought Tsu. She saw his car. It was petrol-driven. 'Very rich,' she said to herself.

'Can't help you, luv,' said the owner.

'But won't the boss come back soon?'

'Can't tell you, luv. Comes and goes as it pleases. See for yourself.'

He jerked a thumb at the boss's keyboard and console. There were no lights lit, no readouts, nothing. Tsu bit her lip. Without the boss machine, no business could be done.

'But you've got meteorites,' she said. 'Some big ones, over there. I want a big one.'

'You've got some money, then, luv?'

'Yes. Have you got a laser?'

'The crew's booked for weeks ahead. And that costs real money. And anyhow the boss is out. Maybe for days.' He cast an appreciative eye at his petrol-driven car. Again Tsu bit her lip. She was getting nowhere.

Then she saw the application form. It lay among a heap of papers and printouts on the owner's untidy desk. It was an Exit form – the form that everyone on Earth filled in; the form that allowed you, if you were very, very lucky, to quit Earth and ship to one of the settled planets. Across the form was printed in big red letters the words SEVENTH REFUSAL.

Tsu licked her lips. She said, 'You want to leave Earth?'

'Yes, luv. Astonishing as it may seem, I want to leave Earth. Join my two brothers out there.'

'You want to leave very much?'

'You could say that, luv.'

'I want a meteorite very much. A big one. That one, there.'

'I dare say you do, luv.'

'And I want a laser crew to do some work on that meteorite.'

'If wishes were horses, luv – '

Tsu reached in her pocket and pulled out her Ident card. 'This is me,' she said, handing the card to the owner of the junkyard.

He looked at the card and whistled.

'That is my father,' she said, pointing to a string of code numbers. 'He's an ACH/VIP. That's a good thing to be.'

'I'm aware of that, luv.'

'I don't think you should call me "luv". You should call me "Miss".'

'You think so, luv? I mean, Miss?'

'If you could help me about that meteorite,' Tsu said, 'I wouldn't be surprised if he could help you about . . . *this*.' She touched the words SEVENTH REFUSAL with the tip of her finger and looked straight into the eyes of the junkyard owner. One of her eyebrows was very slightly raised. 'That would be nice for both of us, wouldn't it?' she said softly.

'I suppose it would, Miss. But how long would you and your dad keep me hanging around for my Emigration permit?'

'How long would you keep me hanging around until the boss is ready to start work? And the laser crew?'

'Well, now. Let's say eight days.'

'Let's say three.'

'Well, three. And what about your side of our little arrangement?'

'Give me five days. I'll have your permit. Oh, by the way: I'll want that meteorite coptered to a place just outside the school. You can't miss it – '

'Ah, well, that's not so easy. Where would I get a copter?'

'Over there,' Tsu said, pointing. The blades of a freight copter were just visible over the piles of junk.

'You don't miss much, Miss.'

'No, I don't,' said Tsu. 'Here's what I want the laser team to do.' She handed the man Ispex's finished drawing.

'Ah, well . . . That's difficult, Miss.'

'So's getting away from Earth.'

'And the boss not here, and all.'

Tsu said, 'I must go.' She smiled prettily at the man. 'Thank you very much,' she said. 'I *like* you. Oh, and don't worry about the boss . . .'

She went to the boss's keyboard and began typing. Nothing happened. She frowned; then smiled again as she leaned behind the machine and touched a tab switch. The console lit up. The boss hummed to itself and began to print readouts. 'Silly old boss,' she said. 'It forgot to switch itself on. Fancy that.'

She left the man scratching his head. Then he murmured 'Ah!' and sat down in front of the boss. He typed in the code number of the girl's father. The boss displayed a screen full of Chinese. The man could not read this. But he could read the one thing that mattered to him. At the bottom right corner of the screen, the luminous letters 'OK' appeared.

He chuckled and began to type out requisitions to his copter and laser teams. 'OK.' Finally he held Ispex's drawing in front of the boss's screen. The boss went *beep*. He took the drawing away and looked at the boss's version of it. The print-out was a web of lines, a complicated lattice: this showed how the boss thought the job should be done.

At the bottom of the screen there appeared 'OK?'

The junkyard owner grinned and tapped out 'OK'

'And that's the last job you'll be doing on this Earth, boss,' he told the machine.

* * *

'You don't mean it!' Makenzi said.

'I do,' Tsu replied. 'The carcase of the ship is to be delivered over there, in the wood. He's going to copter it there. Now we've got to think about the drive units – '

'But how did you get him to swallow all that stuff about your father being an ACH/VIP? I mean, you haven't even got a father.'

'I have on my ident card.'

'But you can't have! I mean, idents can't be tampered with, they're foolproof – '

'I didn't tamper with my ident.'

'Then how – '

'I had it made out East, two years ago, when I was young. I had it carved by hand, letter by letter, from the solid plastic. Then coded inside with chrome-dioxide particles. I don't know if you understand – '

'I do,' Ispex said, looking wonderingly at Tsu. 'Chrome-dioxide . . . !' he murmured. 'When you were young . . . '

Vawn said, 'Wait a minute! You've still got to deliver a permit to him! If he doesn't get his permit, we won't get our meteorite.'

'Oh, I'll give him his exit permit.'

'But how?'

'I'll make it. Draw it. Based on a photocopy from the town. I've got the right paper, that's the only difficult part. I save papers.'

'She saves papers . . . ' Makenzi said, and gave a low whistle.

'But it won't *work*!' Vawn said. 'When he tries to use it, the security people will put it through the coder. They'll know it's a forgery then!'

'*Then*,' said Tsu, coolly, 'yes, they'll know *then*. But, you see, I'll date its validity from – oh, two weeks from now. So he won't try and use it till then.' She lowered her eyes and smiled. 'And by then,' she said, 'we'll be gone. Won't we?'

Nobody said anything because there seemed to be nothing to say. They were stunned. At last Ispex said, 'Wait a minute – *will* we be gone by then? We've got to get drive units and install them and test them – '

Vawn said, 'You told us they'd be easy. You said they were lying around in breaker's yards everywhere.'

'Well, they are. No one uses magnasquids – magnetic scoops – these days, but we could use them. The same with ions and boosts and starters. They're just not wanted, they're junk. But they work. They'd work very well in a tiny ship like ours.'

'But we've got to find them, pay for them, test them,' Vawn said.

'And they've got to be brought to the meteorite,' Makenzi said.

'I'll see they are delivered,' said Tsu, in the small, metallic, chiming voice that always got attention. 'My junkyard man will bring them.'

'How?' Vawn said.

'He's got a copter.'

'Why should he agree to use it?'

'Oh, I'll think of something,' Tsu said. 'Money usually works.' Then, 'I don't like it up here. It's dark and damp and dirty. And anyhow, I've got schoolwork to do. One of us must attend to school duties.'

She went.

THE DRIVES

The three days' detention was over. It was the weekend. They were free to go out and buy the drive units.

They thought it would be difficult. It was not. None of them had fully realised, let alone seen, what 'progress' meant in the twenty-first century.

What it meant was – junk. Every kind of junk. Quaint old television sets with screens only a metre across; the rusting corpses of petrol cars stacked one above the other, covering acres, reaching a hundred metres into the sky; clumsy computer systems and all the hardware and software that went with them; whole spacecraft, with their identification letters and numbers peeling away after fifty years' exposure to the weather; leftovers that no-one wanted to remember in the glittering new worlds where mankind was starting afresh. Junk.

And junked drive units.

'Ion drives over there,' Ispex murmured. He need not have lowered his voice. Nobody wanted the ion units. Anyone could have them at give-away prices. There were whole rows of them, most of them carrying labels saying BOSS-TESTED! GUARANTEED!

They got two ion drives, marked 100 cash, for 160. The boss knocked down the price without even being asked. Obviously all that mattered to the boss was the message it flashed out repeatedly on the screen: BUYER REMOVES * BUYER REMOVES * BUYER REMOVES *

'Now the Maggies,' Ispex said. They inspected the magnetic scoops. The magnasquid units themselves were small, no bigger than half a twentieth-century filing cabinet and much the same to look at. The scoops were big, of course. They were like great gaping mouths with taper throats to the digestive system in the 'filing cabinets'. The mouths picked up space waste, the dust and fragments and detritus – sped them down the throat – and the motor unit translated the waste into power and thrust.

Maggies were slow, uncertain, outmoded drives. But as Ispex said, 'They're good enough for us. They'll *move* us.'

They got two Maggies for 99 cash. The boss would not even take the money until Makenzi had tapped out the collection arrangements on the console. Finally, grudgingly, the boss flashed 'OK'.

A little later, they watched the copters lurch and churn overhead. The grabs came down and picked up their purchases, winched them into their bodies, then chuntered off with them, heading for the wood by the school.

'Suppose someone finds our meteorite and the drives!' Vawn said.

Makenzi said, 'Let someone find them. Who cares? Nobody wants the stuff.'

'I suppose so.'

'I know so.'

Makenzi was right. In the wood, it was all there waiting for them: the meteorite, the size of a small bungalow; the ion drives; the magnetic scoops, one with a battered mouth. Obviously the copter had just let it drop. 'It doesn't matter,' Makenzi said, kicking the mouth roughly into shape. 'The thing is, it's all here! It's all arrived! It's all going to happen!'

'How did you persuade that junkyard man of yours to let us use his copters, Tsu?' Vawn said.

'It was easy.'

'Yes, but how?'

'I fixed his boss.'

'You did *what*? You can't have done!'

'I did. I went there often, without telling you. I hid and watched. I took binoculars. I watched his hands on the keyboard, and the display, and learned the boss code. When the owner was away, I used the boss. It was easy.'

While she was saying this, Makenzi gaped at her. When she finished, he began to laugh. His laughter took hold of him and shook him. He fell to his knees, gulping laughter. 'It was easy!' he said, trying to imitate Tsu's high voice. '*Easy*!' He rolled on the ground, roaring with laughter. 'And there's the poor old owner, watching his copters taking off, flying over his head! – '

'And his boss showing "OK, OK" ' said Ispex. The laughter had gripped him too. He was hiccupping with laughter. And Vawn was laughing, louder and louder. Tsu was calm and silent.

When Makenzi had finished laughing, he

said, 'Do you realise? It's *here*! All of it's *here*! We've actually got it all! – everything we need!'

Ispex said, 'That can't be true, it's impossible. Yet here it is, all of it, the drives, the ship – '

Vawn was gravely dancing in and out of the trees, her arms above her head, her heavy hair flying. 'Epsilon Cool!' she chanted. 'We're coming! Mother, Father, we're coming!'

Tsu said, 'We must remember the navigator.'

'Oh, that,' Makenzi said. 'We'll pinch the school nav, the one in the Science Building, or just follow beams – anything will do, won't it, Ispex?'

'I think so. Yes, anything. Just follow the galactic grid, anything. I just can't believe it, it's all happening, it's all complete – '

Vawn joined them. 'No it's not!' she said. 'It's incomplete. One big thing missing!'

'What?'

'A name! A name for the ship, a name for us! Grand and glorious names!' She whirled away again singing, 'Grand and glorious!'

'She's right,' said Makenzi. 'What shall we name the ship?'

'Trashcan,' shouted Vawn, over her shoulder.

'Bigmouth!' said Ispex, kicking the Maggie scoop.

'Not right, not right,' Makenzi said. 'Wait, wait . . . I feel it coming . . . It's almost here . . . It *is* here!' He leapt on top of an ion drive and flung his hands skywards.

'*Starstormer!*' he shouted. 'I name thee – '

'*Starstormer!*' shouted Vawn and Ispex. Even

Tsu smiled and mouthed the name. Makenzi jumped on to an ion box and began to dance, doing wonderful things with his long thin legs. Ispex imitated him clumsily, his face scarlet.

Vawn cried, 'What about us? What's our name?'

'We're the Starstormers!' Makenzi shouted over his shoulder. 'Obvious! Starstormers, voom! Universe, make room!' He began to sing the words. The others joined in, yodelling the words, turning them into TV commercials, chanting them in three-part harmony.

When they grew tired, they stood watching the automechs, the machines fitting out the ship. They became silent. The automechs were battered, hunched, stained machines that screeched when they probed their drills in the rocky meteorite, squawked when they lifted loads, hummed when they assimilated the new instructions from the boss masterplan. They looked like huge metal woodlice on a piece of rotten wood.

Vawn said what they were all thinking. 'Starstormers!' she murmured. 'We'll be lucky if we get off the ground!'

Ispex replied by turning a careful, clumsy somersault. '*I'm* a starstormer!' he shouted defiantly: and suddenly they were all laughing and singing and dancing again. Above them, pale stars twinkled down tolerantly through a break in the clouds.

'We're coming!' the Starstormers shouted to the stars. 'Mother! Father! We're coming to you on Epsilon Cool!'

EPSILON COOL

'If only they could come,' said Makenzi's mother. One brown finger stroked the rim of the white cup, round and round, round and round. Her eyes looked at nothing. 'If only I could see Mak just for five minutes – just for a minute, Sheila – '

Vawn's mother said, 'Don't start that again, Verona. We made a pact, remember? A pact not to talk about the children all the time. Come on, we'll have another coffee. I'll get them.'

'There's a queue. There's always a queue. And the coffee's horrible. Like everything else.'

Vawn's mother put her thin white hand over the long brown hand. 'Come on,' she said. 'Snap out of it!'

'He'll be enormous by now,' Verona said. 'He's growing up like – like those runner beans we used to have on Earth. Do you remember runner beans? One day *so* high, the next day half way up their poles. Real Earthside things . . . '

'Look, you really must stop it,' said Sheila. 'Be brave and splendid and pioneering, like me!' She pulled a noble face.

Verona laughed and said, 'Well, I am all those things most of the time. We all are. But I don't know . . . when things go wrong, and it seems the settlement will never get settled – ' She waved a hand at the window.

Through it they could see the men, repairing the ecodome. The men wore ecosuits. They had to: the dome was their protection against the dangerous climate of Epsilon Cool. Now the dome was punctured, yet again. How was it punctured? Why was it so often damaged? Nobody knew. But everyone knew what would happen if it wasn't repaired, and repaired fast. The dome came first. The rest of the work still to be done on the settlement had to wait.

'Let's go and see Meg,' Verona said. She stood up, suddenly herself again – tall, slender, sparkling and vivid against the dullness of the canteen. She went to the window and looked out. 'There's Jass,' she said, pointing at one of the ecosuited figures working with the Automechs on the dome. 'Can he see me? Yes he can! Cooee, Jass! Look, he's waving! Silly idiot, he'll fall off if he – and there's your man, Sheila. Dexter. Couple of clowns.'

They waved at their husbands. The men waved back, striking ridiculous poses on the high scaffolding. Verona turned away. 'Time to visit Meg,' she said. 'Come on.'

They went to the sick bay. Meg, Ispex's mother, lay in one of the beds. Her husband Clyde was with her, holding her plump hand. He looked up as Verona and Sheila entered, with relief showing in his eyes.

'And how's the patient?' said Sheila, smiling.

'Impatient,' said Meg. 'I think that's all that's wrong with me, this terrible impatience . . . Clyde, you'd better go, they'll be needing everyone on the dome.'

He left. The women knew he was glad to go, glad to get back to the work that had to be done. 'They're making progress,' Verona said, brightly. 'We were watching them from the canteen. They're doing fine.'

'I'll bet they are,' Meg replied, with a tired smile. 'And they'll do it fine all over again when the dome's smashed up next time.' She began to cry, weakly, then stopped herself. 'And I'm doing fine,' she said. 'The doctor says so. He wants me out. Nothing medically wrong, he says. Well, he's right. It's just this place, this settlement, this prison . . . and not seeing my son, my Jonathan, knowing that if things go on as they are, it could be *years* . . . '

Verona put an arm round Meg's plump shoulders. 'Come on,' she said. 'Our pact, remember? No going broody over our children. None of the mother-hen stuff. One day the settlement *will* be finished and I'll have my Makenzi and Sheila will have her Vawn and you'll have your Jonathan – '

'They call him Ispex, did I tell you that?' Meg said, trying not to cry. 'Yes, of course I told you. A hundred times. It's his *eyes* I'm worried about, I don't trust them at that school, he could be needing a new prescription for the lenses – '

'Listen, Meg,' said Sheila. 'You've got to stop this. Making yourself ill . . . Can't you see, everything's going to be all right, the settlement *will* be finished – '

'And the children,' Verona said, 'they're all right. I just know they are, I feel it. I mean, what can go wrong? They're in that school, which is the right place for them. And they've got friends, they've got each other. Next time the radio works, they'll *tell* you they're all right – '

Meg sat up, her face determined. 'I know, I know, I'm being stupid. Breaking the pact!' She made herself smile. 'Of course they're all right,' she said. 'Of course they are!'

SHAMBLES

The Starstormers made the final checks.

Starstormer was very roughly like a snail and the size of a small bungalow. Inside, the meteorite had been hollowed out in a single spiral, a circular corridor winding in on itself, from which four 'rooms' branched out. The ion drive units were mounted in the last of these rooms, at the rear. They fitted the room so tightly that even if the drives wanted to shake themselves out of the room they could not. Their fuel was sealed bombs of energy, in the centre of the snail, with all the fixed control assemblies.

The Starters were simple rockets. They gave short bursts of power to blast the ship off the ground, out of the Earth's atmosphere. There were stacks of them at four central points in *Starstormer*'s belly.

The mouths of the Maggies, the magnetic scoops, faced forward, gaping at space. It had long been known that there was no such thing as 'empty space': space was full of spacedust, matter shed by the stars, floating debris. The Maggies vacuum-cleaned space. Whatever they caught, big or small, was translated into searing power.

From the outside, *Starstormer* seemed a burned-out, jagged, blue-black cinder left over from fire long dead. She might have been part of a planet on which creatures lived. She might have been anything from anywhere in the universe. Only one thing about her was certain: she was spaceworthy. She had come from space. Now she had the power to return.

Inside, Ispex, checklist readout in hand, checked yet again. The living quarters were simple. Inflatable beds were the main feature. He kicked one bed's feeder switch. The bed went *Oof!* then wheezed and swelled. Fine. He gave the switch another kick and the feeder sucked back its own gas, liquefying it.

'Well done,' Ispex told the bed soberly, and got on with the endless chore of checking. Toothpaste, toilet paper, terrorizers (which went bang and sometimes frightened away the simpler alien lifeforms). Navplan for navigation, Transpeak to translate alien languages, Sunburst for emergency signalling. Glocans for heating food, food for heating in Glocans (the food was simple – half a dozen solids and liquids; a dozen synthetic foods, mostly in tablet form; and rice, rice, rice). Ecosuits –

Ecosuits. He put on his own to check it, making a mental note to insist that the others did so. ('What again?' 'Yes, again.') It was the standard ecosuit, of course, the sort you see in any second-hand shop. The suit took care of you – gave you breath, warmth, vision, hearing, and even light snacks that came through a tube and tasted horrible. It took care of itself, too. Ecosuits were strong. Earthside bullets might kill the wearer of an ecosuit – but the bullets would not hole the suit. The bullets would have to bash you to death from outside. 'But we won't be Earthside,' Ispex said to himself. 'No bullets, just unknown monsters. Presumably they'll eat us whole.'

He went on checking, using the old-fashioned tick method on a readout. He unlatched the door of the Padded Cell, the chamber into which they would crawl during take-off and violent decelerations. He shuddered. It frightened him, partly because of the dimly shining puffy seats with clamps, mostly because he could not understand how things worked. It was all old stuff, forty years out of date. But at least he could operate the check. He ran a hand in front of each clot of sensors: they flashed OK, OK, OK, OK. He shrugged and muttered, 'But how do I know you're really OK?' and stepped backwards, swinging the door closed and feeling its latches grabbing it, sucking it into airtightness.

As he stepped backwards he tripped and fell over a box with some whiskers on it. The box wheezed and said, 'Pardon'.

* * *

Ispex started and said, 'What – ?'

The box again said 'Pardon' and somehow floated over the coke-like floor of the meteorite until it touched Ispex's left leg. Ispex gave a muffled squeak of shock and fear.

The box said, 'GPR mark III reporting for duty.' But then something went wrong with it. The word 'duty' became '*duty-ooty-ooty-ooty-ooty-ooty*', endlessly. Little lights went on and off.

Ispex stared at the hiccuping, hooting box. 'So you're a mark III,' he said to himself, 'a general-purpose robot mark III . . . ' His heart sank. The box was at least five times as old as Ispex himself. It was a relic: a prehistoric monster of a robot. Disgusted, he gave the box a tap with his foot. It said, 'Ooty-ooty-ooty' a few more times, then went 'Dup-dup-dup-dup-dup-dup' and tried to climb a wall.

Vawn was suddenly beside him, laughing helplessly. Now the GPR was doing quite well at climbing the wall. It got all of half a metre up the curve of the dark, laser-cut surface before slipping back again. 'Dup-dup-dup-dup-dup' it said, flashed its little lights and tried again.

'Stop laughing,' Ispex told her. 'Who's responsible for this?'

'Tsu,' she said, still laughing. 'She said she got it cheap. She said it was a bargain.'

'A bargain! That thing!' Ispex said, furiously. Rage flashed from his spectacles. His round face seemed to be tying itself in a tight, furious knot centred on his nose. Helplessly, Vawn laughed.

'It's a disaster!' Ispex said. 'A *cat-as-trophe!* A *shambles!*'

'Dup-dup-dup-dup,' said the box.

'Shambles!' Vawn agreed, weakly through her laughter. 'Oh yes, a shambles! What a perfect name!'

They watched the box, Ispex hopelessly, Vawn helplessly. It was like a very big tortoise with lights on it. It had a head of sorts with whiskery metal feelers sticking out. The head clumsily wagged, the feelers felt. It had six stumpy little legs that tried to row the body up the wall. The legs rowed out of sequence, 1, 3, 2, 1, 3, 2, so that a pair of legs was always doing useful work. That was the idea. The idea did not work on curved walls.

Nor did the machine's other means of propulsion. There was a cushion of air held in by the skirt (it was the air that made Shambles wheeze); and three soft-tyred wheels almost hidden in the underbody.

'He's determined,' Vawn said. 'You've got to give him that. Very determined . . . '

She put her foot under Shambles to help him climb the wall. He got a little higher, then fell over backwards on to her foot. 'Pardon,' he wheezed, then went straight back to the wall, his lights blinking purposefully and his little metallic legs working away busily.

Disgusted, Ispex left, making his way deeper into the spiralling corridor of the ship. Behind him he heard Vawn, still giggling, talking to Shambles. 'You call me Vawn,' she said. 'Do you know your name?'

'Shammm . . . booools.'

'That's right. Now say it quicker.'

'Shammles. Shammle-ammle-ammle-ammle . . . '

'No, *Shambles*.'

'Shamshamshamshamshamshamsham . . . '

'And that's the machine,' Ispex muttered, 'that's supposed to take *care* of us, in space . . . Take care of *us* . . . '

BLAST-OFF

'Are we ready?' Makenzi said. Even if his voice had come from his own mouth instead of through the little speakers built into the Ecosuit helmets, it would not have sounded natural. It was high with anxiety.

'OK,' said Vawn. 'OK' – Tsu. 'OK' – Ispex.

'And your straps are tight? Really tight?'

Another chorus of OKs: and from Shambles, a steady teep-teep-teep. He was in the padded cell with them. 'Why?' Vawn had asked. 'To take care of us if anything goes wrong,' Makenzi had said. She said, 'If anything goes wrong it will most likely be Shambles!' Tsu said, tightly, 'Not now I've attended to him. Me and Ispex.'

Outside, the sun rose over the trees of the wood. The Starstormers saw only a poor TV picture of them. Yet they could see enough. The sun, Earth's sun; the trees, Earth trees: the undergrowth – only a shifting fuzz on the little screen, but real Earth undergrowth, with Earth insects, invisible, leading their tiny, busy lives: and Earth creatures, mice and moles and voles, snails and spiders, sparrows and hedgehogs, earthworms and badgers, all so familiar and real . . .

'This is not real,' Vawn thought. 'I'm not here. This isn't happening. When Makenzi puts his hand on that little console and pushes those little buttons, nothing's going to happen. It's a game, a stupid game, it isn't happening . . .'

Tsu thought, 'Push those buttons. Go on, push them.'

Ispex thought, 'I checked the food and I checked the ecosuits and I checked the Navplan . . . ' But he was only making his mind think like this. His true thoughts were with Mr Whiting. He could see Mr Whiting in his mind's eye, marking them absent. And then there would be reports to the Headmistress and radiomails to his parents – but what did it all matter? Why did he think about these things? All that mattered was that *Starstormer* got off the ground and into space . . . Had he checked the *checklist*?

Makenzi thought, 'I don't want to. I can't. I *can't*.' His hand was like a tendoned claw above the little console. The claw had only to move downwards a centimetre and then – '*I can't*,' he said, actually mouthing the words. Because it was all stupid, childish, babyish. A junk ship filled with four morons and a mechanical clown.

He groaned, brought his fingers down and *Starstormer* exploded.

* * *

Makenzi thought his head had been crushed – that his brain, a scarlet football, had been lit from within with agonising fire. He fainted.

Tsu heard herself scream. She was astonished by the noise and astonished that she could hear it: for the other noise, the explosive noise, was crushing her skull. She fainted.

Vawn thought, 'This is death.' It was not only the unbearable noise, the feeling that her head was being forced into her shoulders, the certainty that her eyes were being forced from their sockets – worse than these was the split-second realisation that her harness had burst. Her hips had slammed down into the soft cushion, bounced up again and torn the lower harness apart. In that split-second, one of her own knees hit her in the face and knocked her out.

Ispex thought, 'This is wrong, two starters have gone off at once!' and then everything was crimson, his eyes were coming out, a bully had smashed him in the face. He fainted.

Shambles, legs splayed, body flattened onto his wheels, said, 'Pardon'.

* * *

One person, Mr Whiting, saw the ascent of *Starstormer*. He saw it through a school window: red and yellow fire, a puffball of black and grey smoke, a dribbling snailtrack of burned air and vapour leading into the sky. A thunderclap; then a distant roar, soon dying. 'So that's what they've been doing,' he said, moodily. 'Idiots.'

He had discovered their absence only half an hour earlier while walking in his dressing gown through the dormitories. He was sleepless, as usual: sleepless because he was a disappointed man, a man without hope, too old to leave Earth, too young not to want to go. 'Idiots,' he said, looking into the dawn sky. 'All be killed. Yet, if I had the guts . . .'

Gloomily, he made his way to the Headmistress's rooms. She would have to be told. Then the authorities, the police, the parents. A lot of fuss. Four stupid kids, probably dead by now. Burned to a crisp, like the last lot. When was that? Ten years ago, eleven? Serve them right.

In the open, the dawn sun made the grass sparkle. He stopped and looked again at the sky, deep blue, luminous, endless, clean.

'Good luck!' whispered Mr Whiting after the starship.

* * *

Vawn came to first. There was a weight on her chest as if a lorry was parked on it. She was afraid to move. But the weight moved. Now it was on her right hip, the right side of her rib cage, inside her right ear. She said, 'Makenzi! Makenzi!'

He heard her, groaned, moved and opened his eyes.

'Makenzi, it's happened! It's worked! We're moving!'

He groaned again and said, 'Hurts . . . ' He woke properly. 'We're moving! We're up! I can feel the weight going round my body!'

Shambles said, 'The ship is rotating,' and blinked some of his lights. He was doing sums. 'We have escape velocity,' he announced.

Vawn, half sobbing with the pain of the constantly moving pressure, undid her top harness. 'Your face!' Makenzi said. 'What hit you?'

'My own knee or something. The lower harness went. I was all over the place, my legs flew up –'

Shambles said, 'Reduction dressing,' and climbed the wall to the medical chest. The wall was netted so he did not slip. He opened the chest with his whiskers and front legs, got a dressing and crawled over Vawn's body. He pressed the dressing to her bruised forehead and nose. Vawn said, 'Ouch!'. Shambles said, 'Pardon'.

Tsu, her eyes still closed, said, 'Why don't we go? We must go!'

Makenzi said, 'We've gone. We're moving. Wake up! Can't you feel the pressure?'

'Oh yes . . . ' Tsu did not groan but the crease between her brush-stroke eyebrows deepened. 'What about Ispex?' she said.

They aroused Ispex. 'We're moving!' he said, immediately. And then, gasping with pain, he was out of his harness and squatting on the floor beside Shambles. 'What's our speed? Acceleration? Rotation? Course? Trajectory?' The questions poured from him. Shambles answered them. The others listened, silently.

At last, Ispex nodded at the TV screen. 'Get us a picture, Shambles.'

Shambles winked his lights. The screen showed flicks and jiggles. 'Pardon,' said Shambles. The images cleared and steadied. They showed a thing, a thing with a curved edge, that almost filled the screen. The thing was grey, green and blue with overlaid pieces of white that made patterns.

'That's Earth,' Ispex said. His voice was hushed.

'Earth . . . '

THRESHOLD OF SPACE

They left the shallow envelope of breathable air surrounding Earth; they entered true space.

They flight-trimmed *Starstormer*, not perfectly but well enough. The ship spun and gave a feeling of gravity in the rooms; but some parts of the corridor near the centre of the ship's mass were sickeningly light and uncertain.

Earth was now a jewelled ball on the TV screen, incredibly remote and unreal. The ball was alive and alight with beauty in its dark setting: it was small and glowing, a jewel to be worn in the hair of the Queen of All the Universe. But it was not their Earth any more, the earth of sparrows and squirrels, rain and sun, Mr Whiting and school food. That world was gone.

'I don't think I care,' said Vawn, when she had looked long enough at the miniature Earth. 'About leaving, I mean. Do you, Makenzi?'

'Pity to miss seeing Mr Whiting's face when he found us gone . . . ' said Makenzi. 'You, Ispex?'

Ispex did not answer. He was crouched over Shambles again, peering at the little lights and readouts, making notes in his checklists.

Tsu said, 'Shambles, get a picture of Epsilon Cool.'

The screen flickered and showed dark blankness. 'No picture available yet,' Shambles said.

'Never mind,' Tsu replied. 'Just hold on that. Forget about Earth. Just look ahead.'

* * *

They ate their first meal in space: a huge meal. Fresh bread, fresh steak, fresh orange juice, fresh vegetables, fresh fruit. 'Eat!' Makenzi commanded. 'Enjoy it!'

'I'm still aching, the pressure . . . ' Vawn complained. 'A bit of steak, perhaps – '

'Eat. You won't eat stuff like this for a long time. Enjoy your food.'

'Yes, sir. Certainly, sir.' She ate, sulkily hiding her face in her hair.

Ispex said, 'Is Shambles getting fed?'

Tsu said, 'Yes, he's connected up to the Maggie. Something might be coming through. But his cells should last for months. He'll be all right. Can I have more potatoes?'

'Vawn's eaten them all. Vawn eats more than any two of us put together.'

'You said "eat",' said Vawn. Her voice was muffled. Her mouth was full of food. She was the thinnest of the four and the biggest eater.

The lights in the little cell-like room went out. Now they were in windowless darkness. Makenzi pressed the button of a Glo and the feeble light lit the curved walls, ridged like the body of a worm where the laser beams had cut.

'Shambles!' shouted Makenzi. There was a distant scuffling and the lights came on again.

'Pardon,' wheezed Shambles. 'I was checking the circuits – '

'That's right, I told him to,' Ispex said. To Shambles, he shouted, 'Did you get any juice from the Maggie?'

'No. Nothing coming through. But I do not need any.'

'He's not a bad old relic,' Ispex said. 'He tries. He is always trying. Very trying.' He chuckled at his own joke.

Vawn said, 'Look, we'll be together for months and months and if you're going to make those *jokes* of yours, Ispex – '

They ate, greedily and splendidly. When they had finished, they cleared up and piled the dishes on Shamble's back. His whiskers and feelers held them. He took the dishes to the Char, the machine that reduced the leftovers to powder and recycled the moisture content. He tried to load the Char but could not. He was not equipped for the job, simple as it was. Makenzi did it for him while Shambles stood by saying 'Pardon'.

Meanwhile Tsu tipped the disposable items down the chute of the Exall, the waste-disposal unit. Steak fat, plastic bottle-tops and paper napkins slid down the chute. She pressed a button. The chute folded into itself and disappeared. Somewhere below there was a metallic noise, the sliding clunk of a door opening; then a hiss, as air from the ship escaped; then a second clunk as the outer door opened and the waste jetted out from the ship. Two more clunks followed. The button Tsu had pressed glowed OK.

Tsu had frowned while all this was going on. She knew about ships that lost all their air through a defect in the Char or its airlock; she knew what happened to the people in the ship. But this Char worked. She stopped frowning and rejoined the others.

PARTY TIME

They were in a good mood – such a good mood that they seemed almost drunk. It was the food, of course: full stomachs. Tsu suddenly caught the infection of good humour. She too began to smile, then to sing. 'Three cheers for the dear old College, it fills you full of knowledge,' they sang, just as they used to a very long time ago, when they were still on Earth. Even Ispex was singing. He was out of tune but he sang loudly, with his round head thrown back and his round nose catching the light and his round mouth a black O –

Shambles was trying to tell them something, flashing his funny little lights, going from one to the other, anxiously pulling at them with his whiskers or feelers or whatever you call them – how absurd, he looked like an illuminated puppy-dog!

'What's your name, Shambles?' Vawn cried.

'Shambles. Please – '

'No, it's not Shambles, it's puppy-dog! Say "puppy-dog"!'

'Puppy-dog. Listen to me, pardon, it's important – '

'It's not *important*, that's not your name, your name is *puppy-dog*! Say "puppy-dog"!'

Vawn was laughing, she couldn't stop laughing. Makenzi was as bad; he was rolling on the floor, roaring 'Puppy-dog!' Ispex was singing. Tsu was shaking his shoulders, shouting, 'No, it doesn't go like that, you've got the tune wrong, *listen*!'

'Oxygen,' said Shambles. 'Please listen – '

'You can't *hear* oxygen,' Ispex said, 'so what's the good of listening? Oxygen is a gas, didn't you learn that at school? I did. "Three cheers for the dear old Coll, it fills you full" – '

'Oxygen!' said Shambles. Now he was turning in little circles, desperately trying to get someone to listen to him. 'Oxygen!' But then something went wrong inside him. He began to go 'Dup-dup-dup-dup-dup-dup . . . ' It was too much. Everyone began to imitate him, choking with laughter, clutching at each other. 'Dup-dup-dup-dup-dup,' they went.

* * *

Vawn, screeching 'Dup-dup-dup', fell. The wall hit her head where her knee had hit it. The pain was so great that it drove out the giddy, drunken feeling. 'What?' she said, vaguely rubbing the pain with her hand but staring at Shambles. 'What?' What did you say? What?'

'Dup-dup-dup-dup-dup-dup . . . ' said Shambles, fastening himself to her ankle.

'Speak properly! Look, press your restart or something . . . Here, let me!' She pressed his restart button.

Shambles said, 'Oxygen.'

'What about oxygen?'

'The mix is wrong. You're not getting enough oxygen. You are suffering oxygen sickness. You are drunk.'

She wanted to stand on her head – everything was going round and round, so why not stand on your head, what's the difference? – but she knew that would be wrong, not good manners, Shambles was trying to tell her something. Be polite! She began to giggle.

'Oxygen! The mix is wrong! Do something!' Shambles insisted. His grasp on her ankle tightened.

'You do it, Shambles,' she managed to say.

'Can't reach. Come with me. Quickly.' He pulled at her ankle. She wanted to oblige him, but now she was sleepy, very sleepy, she could not be bothered. Oxygen? What oxygen? Who where why oxygen? 'I'm going beddy-byes, Shambles,' she said, and giggled. Shambles pulled her ankle. It hurt. She yelped. He pulled again, his metal lashes cutting into her. Grumbling and hobbling she followed him.

He led her down the corridor and towards the centre of the ship. The gravity must be wrong, she kept falling sideways. 'Let go my *ankle*!' She kicked feebly at him. He tightened his grip and led her on.

'Ecoputer,' he said, when they reached the ecoputer.

'What?' she said, staring stupidly at the dials of the machine that computed the craft's climate.

'Correct the levels!' he said. 'Get the needles

all straight, all pointing the same way! Make it say OK!'

She sat down on the floor, staring at Shambles. 'So many little lights,' she said. 'And *you're* covered in little lights. Pretty lights.'

He tightened his grip on her ankle. She yelped with the cutting pain. 'Do it!' he said. 'Pardon, but do it!'

'You're hurting! Will you stop hurting if – '

'Yes. Get up and do it. Now.'

Sometimes frowning, sometimes giggling, she played games with the knobs that made the needles move on the ecoputer. When she lost interest, a metallic thong tightened on her ankle, making her scream.

At last, she said, 'All in line! Simply fine! And there's letters, look, I can see letters, can you see letters?'

'OK,' said Shambles. 'They read OK.' The burning thong round Vawn's ankle loosened its grip. She sighed, rubbed her ankle and said 'What's OK? My ankle – ' Then she slipped to the floor, asleep, one arm pressing down on Shambles's back.

'Pardon,' he said, disengaged the arm, and made his tortoise-like way to the Maggie.

He had saved the Starstormers and their ship. Now he needed some energy, a little recharge.

* * *

Slowly spinning, *Starstormer* went on. Silently spinning, the ship made its way through the near-nothingness of space. Behind her, slowly and silently spinning, Earth receded, a greater jewel among the thousand million jewels of the Galaxy.

Behind *Starstormer*, slowly and silently spinning, followed the ship's attendants – seven bottle tops, two white flasks marked FIZ!, some wrappings and four bones from T-bone steaks; all making their solemn journey through eternity.

OCTOPUS

Time passed. Days, weeks, months. They still used the words but of course they had no meaning. No sun rose and set. No season changed. Time had become timeless: 'a clock-face with no hands', as Ispex said.

For three days, Vawn had put herself into a Big Gloom. She had whimpered, snivelled, then fallen into complete, damp silence behind her curtains of hair. The others were not surprised. Makenzi had said, 'I know how she feels. I wouldn't mind a good long silent sulk myself.'

But now, she had recovered. When Ispex said, 'a clock-face with no hands', Vawn looked up and said, 'But of course, there's got to be time of some kind! I mean, time doesn't stand still. Take us: we're getting older – '

'It's Makenzi's cooking,' Tsu said. He had taken up cooking. Bored with their rations, he crouched over the Glo, mixing this with that and that with the other. But the same old tastes, or lack of them, came through.

Ispex said in his professorish manner, 'Time's relative. I mean, it's not absolute – '

'Oh, dry up,' Makenzi said, wearily. Ispex closed his mouth.

Tsu said to Vawn, 'You're getting fat. You've

just squatted there, sulking and getting fat. I think it's disgusting.'

'Nobody asked your opinion – '

'You should do exercises, like me. I do my exercises every morning and night.'

'Well, hurrah for you. I say, everyone, Tsu does her exercises morning and night, isn't that thrilling?' Nobody answered.

Eventually Ispex said, 'Morning and night – that's what I mean. Time's relative, there isn't any morning or night up here; nevertheless, we've got our watches – '

'Oh, dry *up*,' Makenzi said.

Vawn glowered at Tsu. 'We'll have to call her Tsuper-Tsu, won't we?' she said nastily.

'She'll be fit for anything if she goes on exercising. Or fit for nothing. Because nothing's *happening*, so what's the point of – '

'Something is happening,' Ispex said. 'We're moving through space. We're heading for Epsilon Cool. Aren't we, Shambles? '

Shambles went 'Bip-bip-bip-bip' and obediently started to produce readouts. Ispex greedily followed the readouts displayed on the robot's shimmering, flickering body. No-one else did.

'Don't tell us,' Vawn said. 'Let me guess: only another million, billion, trillion years and we'll be there. On Epsilon Cool, with our parents.'

'If our drives keep driving,' Makenzi said, pulling a face.

'If we don't crash into Tyrannopolis,' said Ispex.

'If we don't get kidnapped by the Octopus

Emperor and eaten alive,' said Vawn.

Tsu said, 'Octopus Emperor! That's horror-comic stuff!'

Ispex said, 'It's not horror-comic stuff! There *could* be an artificial world called Tyrannopolis, because there *have* been signals from it, and star-ships *have* disappeared near where the signals come from! So there *could* be an Octopus Emperor, a pirate emperor, in Tyrannopolis! – '

And all at once, they were no longer bored. Tyrannopolis was always worth talking about, arguing about. And so was the legendary Octopus Emperor, the pirate king of space, the ferocious predator who stole stars and starships –

'Nonsense!' said Tsu. 'You lot believe anything!'

'Pieces of Eight,' said Makenzi. 'Explain them away, Tsu!'

But it was Ispex who explained. He lectured: and for once, they listened. 'We – the human race – *we* never sent those Pieces-of-Eight radio signals,' he began. 'They came from space. A long way out in space. They kept coming – '

'They could have been some sort of joke,' Makenzi said. 'You know, a radio ham fooling about, trying to scare everyone, to create a mystery – '

'Not a funny enough joke,' Ispex said. 'And it's gone on too long. Three years, isn't it? Three years we've been getting those signals . . . Show them, Shambles!'

Shambles showed them. On the curved screens that formed each side of his tortoise-like body, the 'Pieces of Eight' appeared . . . $1+7=8$ $2+6=8$ $3+5=8$ $4+4=8$ $5+3=8$ $6+2=8$ $7+1=8$.

'No, don't show us like that, Shambles. Let's *hear* the signals, the way they first arrived. Do it in beeps.'

Shambles began to beep out the groups of numbers 'Beep – *dick* – beep beep beep beep beep beep beep . . . . DACK.'

Ispex said, 'The "dick" sound is a plus, the long burr is the "equals" sign, the DACK is their sound for eight,' he explained. 'Whoever *they* are . . . '

Shambles went on running through the Pieces of Eight. Vawn shivered. The sounds were cold, alien, somehow sinister.

Ispex said, 'It's the simplest sort of message an alien can send. The aliens don't know our language or even if we have a language. But if we're intelligent enough to do simple sums – well, fine. So *we've* been sending the same sort of thing back into space: the same but different, to show we understand. Show them, Shambles.'

Shambles went, 'Beep-ta-beep, *beepbeep*. Beep-beep-ta-beepbeep, *beepbeepbeepbeep*. Beepbeep-ta-beepbeepbeepbeep-DACK!'

'Twice times table,' Vawn said. 'Twice one is two, twice two is four – '

'Yes, but don't you see, it ends up with their number, eight. Or *his* number – the Octopus Emperor's. So that they know – whoever they are – that we're on the same wavelength, so to speak – '

'But we're not on the same wavelength,' Makenzi said. 'If we were, we'd have got beyond the kindergarten-arithmetic stage. We'd be sending and getting proper messages by now. The Octopus Emperor, or whoever it is out there, would be *saying* something. Something better than beepity-beep.'

'Radio,' said Ispex. 'It could be the fault of our radio. Maybe it's not powerful enough. We get their signals, they can't get ours. You know how our radio is. Take us: we hardly ever manage to get Epsilon Cool. We're cut off from our own parents, even, except for about once a month, when something does get through . . .'

Tsu impatiently interrupted. 'I'm sick of talking about the Octopus Emperor and Pieces of Eight. I vote we try to get Epsilon Cool again. Go on, Shambles – start sending to Epsilon Cool!'

Though they were tired of her bossiness, nobody argued with her. Vawn said, 'Go on, Shambles.' She prodded him with her foot. He changed colour as one bank of little lights went out and another appeared. Humpy and squat, he appeared to be concentrating as he poured out radio signals. The little lights flickered as he tried various frequencies. He hummed and chittered. Numerical readouts told the Starstormers what he was doing. But the light that they were all waiting for, the green light that meant 'Contact established!' never appeared.

The Starstormers' faces grew longer. Vawn sighed. Makenzi bit his lower lip. Ispex pouted and a frown line appeared above his round spectacles. Tsu's face, as ever, was blank; but her fingers pulled unceasingly at the seam of her jeans.

Makenzi said, 'Let's hear what you're hearing, Shambles. Give us the sound.' His voice was blank and without hope. Shambles let them hear what he was sending – the rapid, high-pitched chatter of condensed Morse code; then, without being told, he switched to the signal's echo – the sound bounced back from space. It was sheer noise, meaningless noise.

Savagely, Makenzi imitated it. 'Grack-snap-howl-whine-pop-hoot!' he said. 'Gibberish, drivel, blithering lunacy! And somewhere out there, our parents are – ' Too furious to finish, he threw a plastic mug across the room. It bounced feebly off the curve of the laser-scarred wall and rolled, unbroken, back to his feet. He brought his foot down and crushed it.

Nobody said anything. They stared at the mug, which dutifully tried to resume its proper shape. Silently, it writhed and twisted on the floor. Noisily, Shambles poured out his stream of endless, useless, hopeless radio noise.

'That's enough, Shambles,' said Makenzi, hollowly. 'Cut the cackle.'

'*No, wait!*' It was Ispex who spoke. His eyes, made enormous by the lenses of his glasses, were wide. 'Listen! Can't you *hear*? It could be them!'

They leaned forward, listening. Under the meaningless jumble of sound, you could hear faintly, very faintly, something else: a clean, clear thread of sound: a tiny electronic voice that spoke sense among the chaos: a voice like a thread of water from a tap, the droplets broken so small that the human eye could not follow them, just as the human ear could not take in the outpourings of condensed Morse.

But Shambles could understand. 'Tell us!' Vawn hissed. 'Tell us who it is, Shambles! Is it Epsilon Cool?'

Suddenly the stream of half-heard signals was cut off – and instantly replaced by Shambles's own speaking voice, metallic and rasping.

'I am *Conqueror*,' said the voice. 'I am *Conqueror*. I am the Glory Ark. Who are you?'

THE GLORY ARK

They sighted *Conqueror*, the Glory Ark, two days later. On *Starstormer's* TV screen she was a shape both strange and familiar. Strange, because so ancient – those great blasters, strapped to the side of the hull; that mass of drive units, held together by triangulated girders.

Makenzi whispered, 'It's like coming across the *Flying Dutchman*, or that ghost ship, what was its name?'

'The *Marie Celeste*,' Ispex said. His voice, too, was hushed. 'So old. So strange ...'

But she was also familiar. They could remember TV pictures of such ships. Old people talked about them. And the starship carried Earth registration letters and numbers on her side. She was not alien, simply huge and ancient and unlikely. 'She must be a hundred years old,' Vawn said.

'No, seventy,' Tsu replied. 'GB-7-731. The middle seven is her decadecal, her decade number. A number from the previous century ...'

Shambles interrupted. 'She invites us to dock. What shall I reply?'

'I think OK,' Makenzi said. 'What do we all think?' The others nodded.

Shambles set a new course. Hours passed.

Then the vast old ship was actually before them,

grey and scarred and infinitely complex, sprouting like an underwater wreck with aerials and antennae, barnacled with bumps and lumps of ironmongery and gadgetry –

Starstormer grated and lurched. They had entered *Conqueror's* docking port. There were whistlings and hisses of rushing air as atmospheres interlocked and blended. An amplified voice said, 'Welcome! Welcome!'

The Starstormers walked through a long, dark corridor. They entered *Conqueror*. And for the first time in many months, they saw a fresh human face.

* * *

Fresh, but faded. Their guide was a woman of fifty or more. The flesh of her face seemed to hang on her skull. Her blue eyes were washed out. The skin of her hands was yellow. Yet she moved briskly and her spine was erect. 'I am Sister Monica,' she said. Her smile revealed long, china-white teeth.

'*Sister* Monica?' said Makenzi, when he had shaken her cold hand and introduced the Starstormers.

'Oh yes. Sister. A mere acolyte, a servant, but *they* have honoured me. *They* have risen me in the ranks of Glory . . . '

'They?'

Sister Monica's lips pursed worshipfully. Her eyes looked upwards. 'The Eight of the Elect,' she almost whispered. 'The Gloryseekers! The

Bestowers of Light! The Eight! Surely you know – ah, but of course not, how could you? Follow me!'

She led them through the ship. Following her, they saw that her robe was made from patches of a dozen different materials. In the Meeting Hall, where the hundreds of padded take-off chairs were still used (but their plastic coverings were almost rotted away) they saw the remains of the curtains from which Monica's skirts were made. In the great dormitories – MEN . . . WOMEN . . . CHILDREN . . . MOTHERS – the patchwork bedspreads echoed Monica's bodice. Everywhere paint peeled, plastic surfaces cracked and split, bright metal showed dull, once-cheerful colours were dimmed and fogged.

In one of the three kitchens there was a little scrapheap of pots and pans. Their bottoms had worn completely through. 'We save them, of course, to mend the others,' Monica said, showing her teeth in her tombstone smile. 'We make do and mend. We all help . . . ' She waved her hand vaguely at the people. They were everywhere, yet nowhere: silent, slow-moving, dully dressed, incurious, always seeming to be on their way somewhere else.

'How many people are there aboard *Conqueror*?' Tsu asked.

'*Conqueror*? Oh, you mean the Glory Ark . . . Some seven hundred and twenty souls, my dear. All bound for Glory.' The smile.

'How many were there when the ship left Earth?'

'Five hundred. Exactly five hundred. So you

see, we thrive, we prosper. We increase and multiply.' Her smile invited an answering smile. 'I myself am a grandmother. An infant Glory-seeker was born only two days ago . . . ' She made a sign over her chest, a quick, double-circular movement.

'Figure of Eight,' Vawn whispered to Ispex. 'But why?'

Ispex hissed, 'Obviously because – ' But Monica herded them forward: forward to the Climate Room (KEEP OUT), the Drive Complex (KEEP OUT), the dining rooms (GS ONLY), the bathrooms (GS ONLY).

'GS only?' Makenzi asked.

'Gloryseekers only,' Monica explained, smiling.

'But which people *aren't* Gloryseekers?' Vawn said. 'I mean, who is there aboard who's *separate* from people like you?'

Monica's smile faded. Her eyes became round with nervous awe. 'Why, there's – them,' she said. Her voice was hushed. She pointed a finger upwards. '*Them.*'

'Them?' Vawn said. 'You mean, the crew? The Captain and the crew?'

'Well, yes,' Monica replied, uncertainly. 'The Captain, the crew. They *were* that, before the Glory came . . . '

'I want to see them,' Makenzi said, abruptly. 'Are they up there? Where this lift goes? Shall we take the lift and go and see them?'

Before Monica could stop him, he had pressed the lift button. The sign above the button reading NOT FOR USE OF GS PERSONNEL suddenly lit up and buzzed angrily. 'No! You don't understand! – ' Monica began, trying to pull them back, but the lift doors were opening, the clean, bare chamber accepted them, the doors were closing.

'No!' said Monica: and the doors closed in her face.

The lift rose. There were no buttons to press, no choices to make. The lift took them – stopped – opened its doors – and blankly invited them to get out. Facing them was a huge sign, two metres high: a sign like a spider, or perhaps an octopus; a double circle with legs sprouting from the place where the circles met.

'Eight,' said Ispex. His mouth pouted. The others knew he was thinking hard. 'Always eights.'

'What do you mean?' Makenzi began, but a voice from nowhere interrupted. 'This way,' it said. 'This way. That's right.'

It was the pleasantest voice imaginable: deep, masculine, kind, amused. They followed it, making their way through what seemed to be a maze of glass walls, glass corridors, glass everywhere, glittering and reflecting back on itself, completely confusing . . .

But the voice guided and welcomed them.

THE GLORIOUS ONES

They were in a glassy room the size of a small office. 'There!' said the voice. 'Delighted to meet you!'

'But where?' Makenzi said. He could see no-one. Yet the voice was close to him, very close indeed.

'Stupid of me,' said the voice cheerfully. A light grew from a golden glow to a bright, all-enveloping haze: and there he was, the speaker, smiling at them, holding out his hands in welcome. 'What an amazing bunch you are!' he said and smiled more broadly.

He wore a uniform, old fashioned but still recognisable – the uniform of a Starship Captain; the Starstormers saw three gold bands round his upper arm, and the wide gold bands on his shoulder straps. His face was that of a very old man who had stayed young. His hair was like the finest filaments of white nylon but the skin of his face was firm. Hundreds of fine wrinkles around his eyes made him seem to smile; and when he did smile, his mouth and chin gave an impression of good-humoured energy. Only an impression: because the glass somehow clouded him, the layers of glass got in the way, the glass was everywhere –

'Who are you?' said Vawn, her face alight with pleasure.

'Who are you?' said Ispex, his lips still pouting and his voice gruff with suspicion.

'Captain Shander at your service. Very much at your service! That amazing ship of yours, do you mean that you've actually travelled from Earth in it?' He leaned forward, the fingertips of his strong hands resting on one circular half of his double desk. A TV picture of their ship was on the wall.

Makenzi started to explain about *Starstormer*. Ispex cut through. 'Where are your Officers?' he demanded.

Captain Shander said, 'Oh, I was going to introduce you later, but if you wish – '

The golden haze extended and deepened. Through the layers of glass, the crew became apparent: seven officers. Two of them young, in their twenties; the others, like their Captain, apparently very old – yet amazingly well preserved. The Officers waved, smiled and returned to their work.

'Busy,' said Captain Shander. 'Always busy, as you can see. If they weren't, they'd want to welcome you properly – shake you by the hand – '

'I'd like to shake your hand,' said Ispex. His voice and face gave the lie to his words. His lower lip stuck out. He was glaring. He thrust out his hand. 'Shake hands!' he said.

The other Starstormers watched Ispex in amazement. The charming Captain merely smiled. 'Indeed, I wish I could!' he said, 'But there are certain difficulties in the way.' He laughed and tapped a sheet of the glass surrounding him. The little sound seemed to boom and echo like distant drums.

'Why the glass?' said Ispex, still astonishingly rude.

'Ah, I see what's worrying you,' the Captain said, and sat down in his chair, taking his time. It was interesting to see him make this simple action: interesting the way the glass – there was so much glass – seemed to make the gold rings on his arm shimmer and jump. But he sat; and smiled; and explained.

'I am a hundred and eleven years old,' he said – then grinned, almost boyishly, at their amazement. 'Yes, I am the original Captain of this ship. I was thirty-nine when the voyage began. Most of my passengers died half a century ago. The people you have seen today are the sons and daughters and grandchildren of the original voyagers –'

'Why the glass?' Ispex insisted. Vawn muttered 'Ispex! Behave!' and pulled at his sleeve. But Ispex stuck his head forward and repeated, 'Why the glass?'

Captain Shander smiled. 'Why the glass? To isolate me and my Officers, completely, from everyone else on the ship. You see, it was known and expected that the settlers would be replaced by their own children; that was and is the purpose of the flight – to resettle other planets with humans. But it was thought essential that the Senior Officers, like the ship itself, should endure.

So some of us were given the gift – if it is a gift – of long life. And to protect our lives, to isolate ourselves from ordinary human illnesses, we have had to cage ourselves in. To isolate ourselves. It has been a lonely, difficult existence . . . but the sacrifice had to be made, the voyage had to succeed –'

Ispex said, 'That's a nice desk you've got.' His voice was as surly and rude as ever. This time Makenzi pulled at his sleeve. 'Shut up, Ispex.' Ispex sullenly tugged himself free of Makenzi's grasp and said, 'A nice desk. Two circles, joined together. Like the design facing the lift. Sort of eight-shape. Octopus-shape.'

'Hope,' said the Captain. 'A simple symbol of Hope. I like it, don't you? One circle represents our own world, dear old Mother Earth; the other circle stands for the new world, the world we must eventually reach . . . But always the links will remain. Always the two circles will be linked . . .' His voice had softened. His words sounded almost poetical. Even Tsu was affected.

'The old and the new,' he murmured, 'Apart, but always joined . . . Joined by us. Humankind.'

'Glory, Glory, Glory,' said Ispex, bleakly.

'I beg your pardon?' said Captain Shander.

'Glory,' said Ispex. 'There's a lot of Glory about in your ship.'

The Captain laughed, gently. 'Oh, I see what you mean,' he said. 'Sister Monica, and the others . . . Is it surprising? Does religion shock you? I suppose it does, you are very modern young people . . . These people, the settlers, are perhaps not as up-to-date as you are. And they are isolated. As the years went by, and the decades, and even the half-century, they found a religious purpose for themselves. They came to see their voyage as an argosy, a journey towards Glory. Is that so very wrong, do you think?' He smiled quizzically at Ispex. Ispex said nothing. He pouted.

'Well, *is* it wrong? ' said Tsu, sharply.

'Tell us, Ispex!' said Vawn.

One of the Officers, a woman, materialized through the golden haze. She spoke in a low voice to the Captain. 'You must excuse me,' he said to the Starstormers. 'I had forgotten. Quite shortly, I must appear before the people. They seek Glory: they get – me.' He smiled modestly, charmingly.

'We'll leave,' said Makenzi, politely.

'As you wish. Explore the ship! There's so much to see and we can meet again later – ' The Captain turned away and joined his Officers. Again, there was a shimmering effect to his movements, a slightly ghostly fading as he entered the deeper gold of the haze behind him.

'Come on,' said Makenzi. They left.

They stood waiting for the lift to ascend. Vawn was the first to explode. 'Of all the piggish, stupid, moronic, ill-bred – ' The words poured out of her mouth and into Ispex's ear.

'You're a lout,' Tsu said.

'You ought to have your backside kicked,' said Makenzi. 'In fact, when we're alone, I'll see to it.'

Ispex seemed not to hear. He said, 'We've got to get out of here. The quicker the better.'

'Get out? We've only just got here! Why – '

'You don't *think*,' Ispex said. 'If you thought, you'd see it all. We've got to get out!'

The lift came.

THE GLORY SEEKERS

Sister Monica was waiting for them at the bottom of the lift. Her eyes flickered uncertainly but the tombstone smile was fixed on her face. 'You were very naughty, running away like that,' she said, 'very, very naughty. Now follow me. And this time, *stay* with me.' She wagged a roguish finger at the Starstormers.

They followed her in a silence only broken by Ispex's mumblings. 'Don't you see,' he muttered in Makenzi's ear, 'don't you see, we've got to escape! Soon!' Makenzi shrugged him off.

They found themselves part of a silent crowd, all heading in the same direction and all with serious faces. As the people walked, the women and girls put on strange little bonnets: the men and boys pinned what looked like football favours to their chests.

Vawn whispered to Monica, 'What's happening?'

As Monica replied she adjusted her own bonnet. 'You are fortunate, my dear,' she said, tying the bonnet's strings under her chin. 'You are able to join us in the most meaningful – ' (she tugged the strings) – 'most uplifting – ' (she tied the bow) – 'most significant occasion of our week!' (Now the bonnet was in place and the smile widened to show more little tombstones.) 'We join to give *praise*,' said Monica, her eyes milky with devotion, 'praise to those who guide us to Glory. Glory, Glory, Glory . . . !'

'But who are the guides? And *what* Glory?' Vawn spoke too loudly. Heads turned to reprove and silence her. Mouths pursed. And as the heads turned, Vawn began to giggle. For on top of each female head were the bonnets: and the bonnets resembled nothing so much as – what was the word – *brassieres*, that was it, those things women wore in the twentieth century. Little brassieres, perched on each head – a white or pink blob above one ear, a blob above the other ear! The giggles rose in her throat. Monica's bonnet was pink, pretty pink, and the long, solemn face beneath it was so earnest and solemn . . . The giggles pulled and tugged at Vawn's stomach and windpipe, bubbling and jumping, determined to escape –

They were in the place of worship now, the huge hall, the biggest chamber in the Glory Ship. Vawn could not take it in – the giggles were surging up and the faces under the double-bubble, Minnie Mouse, brassiere bonnets made it all the worse, they were so *solemn* – and everyone seemed to be making the double-wiggle sign over their chests –

She knew that the best way to control giggles is to stare deliberately at the ceiling. This ceiling was low and covered entirely in pipes. Square pipes, round long pipes, thin pipes, fat pipes, pipes with peeling paint, pipes showing rashes of rust, sombre pipes that fed the ship, important pipes doing their duty . . . Vawn thanked them as her giggles sank back in her stomach.

Ispex's voice in her ear said, 'We've got to get out, don't you *see*,' but she concentrated on the pipes. Everyone was singing, it sounded like a hymn, but she stared at the pipes. A voice, badly amplified, said, 'Glory! They are coming! Glory! They are nigh!' and the congregation rustled and stirred. Vawn felt it safe to drop her eyes: she wouldn't giggle. She looked around her.

She saw the altar. Glass, it was only glass, glass luminous and golden, growing brighter, sheets of glass with a squiggle engraved on them, the same squiggle that the people made over their chests, a squiggle that reminded her of the double-circle of the bonnets (but better not think of them, the giggles might start again). She looked at the glass and became interested.

The congregation rose to its feet. Now the glass was very bright, and there seemed to be things inside it or behind it, glowing things . . . '*We've got to get out*!' Ispex said in her ear. She turned her head away. The things became plainer and plainer, it was exciting, the music was getting louder, too, and the loudspeakers were shouting, 'Glory – Glory – Glory!'

So that was all the things were! People. The Officers.

She could see them plainly now although they were behind so many layers of glowing glass: the Officers, sitting on gold chairs, wearing white uniforms, all smiling and slowly nodding their heads. Sister Monica, hands clasped, was bent forward, crying, 'Glory! Glory! Glory!' There were actual tears falling down her cheeks.

The noise became deafening, the old loud-speakers crackled and produced split notes – 'GLORY GLORY GLORY!' and now Ispex was shouting in her ear. He could safely shout: he was yelling, 'Quick! Follow me! OUT!'

'No,' Vawn said, 'This is terrific, I'm staying.'

'*I'm going*!' He seized her arm and pulled so hard that she was forced to her feet. '*Come on*!' he said and tugged again and she half fell against people. 'No!' she said – but now Makenzi was pulling at her too and they were in the aisle. No-one noticed them but Sister Monica. They saw her turn and reach out a hand, uncertainly. Her mouth shaped the words 'Come back!' but Ispex said, 'Come *on*!'

'All right, all right! But where's Tsu?'

They spotted her. She was on her feet, making the sign. Her eyes were fixed on the altar. Her lips were parted.

Ispex and Makenzi grabbed her arm and pulled her into the aisle. The four of them began walking, fast. They left the great chamber. Nobody followed them but they saw Sister Monica look back, her long face working with confusion and worry.

'Quick!' Ispex said. 'We've got to get out! Get them to *Starstormer*!' They could only half-run: Tsu held them back. Her eyes stared at nothing. Her lips said, 'Glory!'

None of the doors was locked. A voice shouted 'Stop!' but they ignored it. They found the docking corridor leading to *Starstormer* and ran down it, dragging Tsu.

Shambles let them in. He chittered and beeped at them. Ispex shouted 'Out! Away! Get us out!'

He and Makenzi ran round *Starstormer* setting her up. Shambles attended to the electronics and numericals. 'Status Off!' he squawked.

The blasters bellowed and *Starstormer* gave out a ring of yellow, red and purple fire that exploded against the flanks of *Conqueror*. Then the little meteorite ship was away, sidling into the infinite darkness, and only her smoke remained, crawling lazily over the intricate sides of the ancient starship.

'What was all that about?' Vawn demanded. 'What was the panic? It was just getting interesting!'

'Real-vision,' Ispex said to Shambles. 'Can you set the ship up to give me real-vision?'

'But there's nothing to *see*,' Vawn said. 'Only *Conqueror* – '

Makenzi said, 'Quiet. Ispex was right, I've been working it out . . . What *do* you expect to see, Ispex?'

'I don't know. Either nothing, or something spectacular.'

The two of them put their heads together at the real-vision panel, a small block of armoured glass that, thick as it was, was the weakest part of the meteorite hull. They stared out. There was *Conqueror*, receding very slowly from their view, but still so big that she more than filled the RV glass. Behind them, Vawn, trying to see, complained, 'You might explain! What was all that panic about? Tsu, do you know?' But Tsu was silent, crouched in a corner.

Over his shoulder, Ispex told Vawn, 'Surely you see? Pieces of Eight! The Octopus Emperor! The *people* were all right – the settlers, the passengers – but the *Officers* . . . And all those Eight signs – '

Even as he spoke, it happened. The RV glass seemed to explode with blazing light. Ispex and Makenzi flinched back, then craned forward, their heads pressed against the glass. *Starstormer* shuddered and rocked as the shock waves hit.

Conqueror was exploding.

The first and greatest explosion came from the centre of the ship. It was a ball of violet fire, red-edged, that blossomed out with horrible slowness – then suddenly accelerated and became an enormous flower of fire in the blackness, a flower with many-coloured twisting petals and grey-blue leaves of smoke. The mighty hull was almost hidden for perhaps five seconds; then the flower died and the petals scattered, slowly, fading as they flew, and the leaves of smoke rushed outwards.

'She's broken in half!' Ispex whispered.

Now smaller flowers, just as horrible, began to bloom and burst. The broken hull seemed to shed parts of itself with each explosion. Great torpedo-shaped drive units glowed with inner fire, spouted torrents of brilliant flame and tore from the ship. They spun and spiralled through the dark nothingness, lit with bulging orange flame and livid corkscrews of smoke that was itself alive with fires and starbursts of burning metals and chemicals.

The great hull twisted its broken back and began to topple on its side like a wounded animal. Ragged metal twisted and tore as if the dying body was showing its skeleton. Little explosions, innocent-looking after the first great fireball, made luminous boils on the flanks; the boils burst and spat fire and metal and things that one could only guess at . . . dark, writhing things that flailed against the brightness of the fire, then disappeared.

Makenzi said, 'I can't watch this,' and dropped his head. But then there was a roar, a yell, that shook the sky and something dark yet bright howled by, tossing *Starstormer* like a dinghy in a great sea; and Makenzi looked again. 'What was that?'

'I don't know,' Ispex muttered. 'One of her drive units, perhaps. If it had hit us . . . '

Now the blazing wreck was dropping parts of herself. The pieces dropped in any direction – there was no gravity, no 'down' to 'fall down' on. 'Get us out!' Makenzi whispered hoarsely, 'Shambles, get us moving!' As he spoke, his face was still at the RV window. He could not tear himself away.

The nose cone of the doomed starship lifted itself like a rooting snout, tore itself from the hull and fell upwards, very slowly. The Starstormers – all four of them were fighting for a place at the RV glass now – saw the cone swing outwards, revealing a honeycomb of cells and a thousand little threads of metal.

'The pipes,' Vawn said, 'I suppose those must be the pipes I was looking at . . . ' She shuddered, thinking how big the pipes had looked, how threadlike they seemed now. The cone, tethered by the lattice of pipes, swayed languidly, like a jellyfish. Little objects fell out, spinning away, to be swallowed by the blackness all around. Some spurted fire as they fell. Pieces of metal, twisting and spinning, came lazily at *Starstormer*, then seemed to accelerate and hurtle past –

Suddenly the RV glass was dark, and the Starstormers found themselves falling over each other, clutching each other. Everything seemed to spin. Vawn screamed, 'We're hit!' Shambles' voice said, 'No. I gave the ship max boost.' Ispex said, 'It's all right, we weren't hit – '

As he spoke there was a dull thump from somewhere. 'We *were* hit,' Ispex corrected himself. 'Flying debris. Can't have been anything very big. Just as well . . . Where are we going, Shambles?'

'Away. Fast. A course can be decided later.'

Starstormer spun in space. Sometimes *Conqueror* could be seen, but now no-one could bear to look at her for long. Part of her was burning. In front, the nose-cone still dangled and little rivulets of fire and explosions ran along the web that held the cone to the hull. Once the Starstormers heard but did not see another great explosion and the RV window, though not facing the ruined ship, lit up. Nobody looked. Nobody spoke.

At last, Makenzi said, 'All those people . . . ' Vawn said, 'All the settlers, hundreds of them. All dead. And the Officers, too . . . '

'The Officers?' Ispex said. 'I wouldn't worry about them. They're not dead.'

'They must be! The ship was ripped apart! What do you mean, not dead?'

'You've got to be alive before you're dead,' said Ispex. 'You didn't think those Officers and the Captain were *alive*, did you? You didn't think they were *real*?'

Ispex explained. By now, the *Conqueror* was a dull glow in space, a thousand miles behind them. By now, they were on course once again for Epsilon Cool, and the ruin of the old starship and the horror of its death were no longer so dreadful. They ate their suppers and listened to Ispex, amazed.

'I'm surprised you didn't see it,' he said. 'It was obvious. But then, you don't *think*, not *really* think . . .

'The Pieces of Eight – the Octopus sign – those double-bubble bonnets – how could you miss it? That great big sign outside the lift; and the way people crossed themselves, with that special double-circle sign – well, I saw it straight away. The people had been brainwashed – no, that's too strong, *educated*. Educated for years and years. Taught, first, that the crew, the Officers, were supermen, better than themselves, little gods . . . I suppose the crew cut themselves off from the rest and lived a special sort of life in their own quarters. And people died, and had children, and the years rolled on and on, and a sort of religion must have started, with the Officers as the High Priests, something like that . . . '

'But you said the Officers weren't real, they weren't human,' Vawn said.

'They were at first. But someone on board that ship must have been a traitor – a secret agent of the Octopus Emperor. Oh yes, I know it sounds silly, but it must have been that way, just *think*! Because what happened was this. Somehow – don't ask me how – the Octopus people (if they *are* people) got aboard, or came out of hiding, or whatever they do, and they killed the Officers and crew. Did away with them, made away with them. And they replaced the dead men with – '

'Themselves,' said Makenzi, wonderingly. 'Of course! And that's why there was all that glass – '

'So that you could never *see* them properly,' Ispex said. 'Because, you see, there was nothing to *see*! There was no Captain! There were no Officers! There was nothing but images, pictures, ghosts on glass!'

'Impossible,' said Tsu. She had been listening to Ispex uneasily, pulling at the seams of her clothes. Her face was sulky, resentful. 'Impossible!' she said again. 'I mean, how do you create your stupid images?'

'Holograms!' said Ispex and Makenzi, simultaneously.

'Yes, they were holograms,' said Ispex. 'They must have been. Why else all the glass? They were simply cinematic holograms, moving solid pictures – '

'But why did the real people *accept* them?' Vawn said.

'Because they wanted to. They were looking for something, anything. The Octopus people introduced that Glory-Glory religion: the people were excited, thrilled, lifted up by the mystery and excitement and promise – '

'Why, why, WHY?' Tsu said, almost shouting. 'What's the point of it all? Even if you're right, what's it all *for*? You rave on, Ispex . . . Pieces-of-Eight, the Octopus Emperor – ha, ha! – holograms and traitors and all the rest of it . . . I tell you this: if I were an invading force, I wouldn't dress myself up as a hologram and do stupid things in an out-dated spaceship! I wouldn't spend half a century messing about with ordinary humans!'

'I don't know why,' Ispex said glumly. 'But it's obvious they *wanted* the humans – '

Makenzi said, 'Yes, but why blow up *Conqueror*? Because it must have been them, the ship didn't just *happen* to go up when it did!'

'Why?' Ispex said. 'Because the game was up, that's why! Once some human discovers that the Captain and the Officers are fakes – well, it's all over, isn't it? *We* know: we'll be reaching Epsilon Cool one day, and we'll tell people what we know. And even if we never get there, we'll be in touch with humans with our radio, we'll be telling people what we know. It might be tomorrow, even, that we tell people, real people, our people – '

'If they let us,' Makenzi said, soberly.

'What did you say?' Vawn asked, her eyes wide with fright.

'If they let us! You understand me, Ispex, don't you?'

'Yes. Oh, yes. Look, Vawn, they blew up *Conqueror* to get rid of the evidence of what they're doing. What do all the dead people on *Conqueror* matter to the Octopus Emperor? He doesn't care! The experiment hasn't worked, blow it up! But that leaves – *us*. We escaped. We escaped *from* something all right. But what have we escaped *to*?'

The others looked at him blankly. Vawn said, 'You mean, we're the next ones on the list? The Octopus lot will be going for us now?'

'I would be if I were them,' said Ispex. 'But perhaps . . . I mean, we're very small fry, the ship's tiny, we're children. Perhaps we'll get away with it. Just possibly we'll – '

Shambles, lights flashing, entered the room. He ran in circles. His lights flashed meaninglessly. He could not find his proper voice until Makenzi, sensing serious trouble, pushed his Cancel buttons and restarted him. Then Shambles spoke, his voice calm and harsh in the little room.

'*We are being attacked*,' he said.

THE FIRST INVADERS

The four Starstormers seemed frozen: Vawn and Tsu standing, Ispex crouched, Makenzi bent over Shambles. 'Attacked?' said Makenzi. 'How? By what?'

'Attack! Attack!' Shambles said. His voice was harsh and decisive, yet his actions were absurd. He was trying to run in circles. His displays and lights were running riot. But one cluster of lights showed something definite. Ispex studied them and said, 'There's something in the ship, or trying to get in. Shambles has never shown anything like this before.'

Makenzi said, 'We'd hear something, feel or see something,' and flicked through the ship's TV programmes. The screens showed nothing on or near *Starstormer*.

Tsu ran to the RV window. 'Nothing to see,' she said.

Ispex knelt by Shambles, tapping out numerical questions on his side. 'Nothing,' he reported. 'He just keeps saying we're being attacked.'

Then Vawn spoke. She stood bolt upright, her arms by her side, her eyes unfocussed and staring straight ahead. She said, '*We are being attacked.*'

The others shouted questions at her. They pulled at her arms. She did not look at them. '*They are in the ship,*' she said.

'What's in the ship? Where?' they demanded.

'*Everywhere*,' she said, dully. Suddenly her eyes became wild. She began to strike at the air with clawed hands. She shouted. '*Keep them out!*' she screamed. '*I hate them! Keep them away from me!*' She fought when they tried to hold her. '*Flies!*' she screamed. '*Little flies! Keep them off me! Please, please!*' Her clawed hand hit Makenzi's face. Her nails cut his cheek. Blood came out in little blobs that ran together.

'Help me, Tsu!' he gasped. 'Take her other arm! Help me get her strapped down!' The two of them got her to the Padded Cell, the take-off chamber, and strapped her down.

'*My face!*' she screamed. '*They're on my face! Cover my face!*' They covered her face. She sobbed and struggled under the covering.

'I'll stay with her,' Tsu said. 'You go back to Ispex and Shambles. Find out what's happening.'

Makenzi found Ispex prodding at Shambles' sides. 'I've tried everything,' Ispex said. 'Can't get any sense out of him. He insists we're being attacked – '

'So does Vawn,' Makenzi said, grimly.

'What do we do?'

Makenzi bit his lip. 'I don't know,' he said at last. 'No, wait! I do! Try to get through to Epsilon Cool!'

'But that won't help us!' Ispex began.

'It might help *them*,' Makenzi replied. 'Don't you see? If we've had it – if we really are being attacked by something we don't understand and can't fight – at least we can warn other people, at least we can tell our parents what they might have to face – '

Ispex said, 'You're right. Shambles, try for Epsilon Cool. Try all the frequencies.'

The machine was still almost frantic. It chattered, 'We won't get through, it's all noise – '

'Try.'

Makenzi and Ispex listened to the noise. It was the noise of space, the meaningless scrabblings and roarings and whistlings and thin screams from nothing and nowhere; the sounds of a non-existent zoo, with shrill, invisible birds in the aviary and great formless beasts roaring and howling at eternity from barless, dimensionless cages.

Makenzi shook his head at Ispex. 'Hopeless,' he said.

And then the zoo was suddenly gone, and a human voice, matter-of-fact, a little bored, said, 'Well, take it up with the Commissary, I can't deal with it.' A female human said, 'Don't try that on! You've got the requisitions, deliver the goods!'

'Epsilon Cool,' said Shambles.

'My father!' Makenzi said, choking the words. 'Get me my father or mother! Get them for me! Quick!'

CONTACT

Three hours later, when all the loving words had been spoken, and even Vawn had talked with her parents (though she constantly brushed at her head, trying to clear away the invisible flies), the radio link with Epsilon Cool was finally broken. The non-existent zoo took over again. The beasts roared, the birds screamed. The Starstormers were once again on their own. But they had delivered their warning.

Makenzi said, 'Recap. Let's tell each other the things that matter most for Shambles to record and sort out. Vawn, are you all right?'

She brushed aside the invisible flies and said, 'Yes.' Her face was haunted. 'My mother,' she said, 'I heard her voice . . . '

Makenzi said, gently, 'We'll talk about that later. Now, we've got to talk about what we're going to do. What's happening to us. Ispex, you start.'

Ispex said, 'Well, the flies. Whatever they are, they're not flies. They seem to be particles, like dust. Our parents knew about it, didn't they? All those other cases of people in starships being attacked by "flies" . . . '

'But what *are* they?' Vawn said. There were tears in her voice. 'Why am I the only one to – '

'We don't know what they are,' Ispex said. 'We

do know that you're the only one sensitive to them. You seem to feel them, we don't. But it seems that they're the attackers, the invaders. We know they're here. We don't know how to deal with them. Nobody does.'

'What happens?' Vawn said. She was crying now, feebly. 'What are they going to do to us?'

'Nobody knows. They can't touch us, I suppose – not do anything, like hitting us, or taking over the ship – '

'They can,' Vawn sobbed. 'I can feel them. They can do anything they want to do. Can't you feel them touching you? Can't you *smell* them?'

Nobody dared answer. By now, all of them sensed the presence of the flies, the particles. It was as if there were another person in the room, a powerful person, a silent enemy. And then there was the smell: the faint, odour of – what?

'Hot metal,' Vawn said. 'It's a hot-metal smell. You *must* be able to smell it!' The wings of hair hid her face. Tears dripped from the wings. Tsu stroked her shoulder.

Nobody answered Vawn. There was nothing to say. Each could smell hot metal.

Tsu said, 'All right, that's enough about *them*. We can't do anything about them so what use is talking? What about the meet-up? Have we got that sure and certain?'

'Yes,' said Makenzi. 'We checked and double-checked. You heard. Tell us again, Shambles.'

Shambles changed colour, beeped and began to recite, 'Meet-up with Epsilon Cool personnel two Earthside days from now, 1600 hours. The

Epsilon Cool shuttle ship adjusts to our course which is . . . ' He chittered and beeped, working out and correcting *Starstormer*'s heading. The Starstormers let him get on with it. They thought of their parents. In two days, they would be with their parents. In only two days . . .

Shambles recited, '173, trajectory eleven, acceleration fourteen o nine, counter-G fifteen seven twelve . . . ' Ispex tried to listen but – soon, very soon, the ship from Epsilon Cool would be there, actually there, and inside it his parents –

He pulled himself together and said, 'So we're OK on course, Shambles? And you don't see any trouble with the meet-up or the docking?'

'Epsilon Cool's shuttle will control the meet-up and the docking. No problems.'

'No problems,' Ispex said, looking from one to the other of the Starstormers, his face plump with satisfaction. Then he caught the faint aroma of hot metal. His face fell. He looked at Tsu's face, so cool and private; no parents for her.

Ispex pouted, then began to bite his lower lip.

* * *

The first day of waiting somehow passed.

The smell of hot iron became stronger. Afraid to confess their fears to each other and ashamed of being afraid, the Starstormers separately peered in dark corners, lay awake and listened for noises, sniffed the air and then pretended their noses itched.

Vawn ceaselessly brushed at the 'flies'. But

already the gesture had become automatic. The cloud had left her face. Now she spoke only of tomorrow, and her parents. 'It will all be over tomorrow,' she said. 'I can't wait for tomorrow . . . '

Makenzi and Ispex worked as a team with Shambles, checking and re-checking course and trajectory, ecosuits and dock latches, auto-systems and their manual over-rides – everything. When the time came, they intended that nothing would go wrong. The two ships would meet and dock. The latches would grab and lock on, the two atmospheres would hiss and mingle; and then *they* would be there, their parents . . .

Tsu remained Tsu: withdrawn and private, cool and small, neat and tight. Makenzi said, 'Only another day, Tsu, and then – but of course, it's different for you, not having parents . . . We all realise that and we're all sorry . . . '

'That's all right,' said Tsu, her voice cool and high.

'What I was trying to say was –'

'I understand,' said Tsu. 'It's quite all right. I will cut your hair ready for tomorrow, it looks ridiculous. Fuzz everywhere. Sit in front of the mirror.'

'Thank you, Tsu. Thank you very much.'

'That's all right.'

She cut his hair. In the mirror, he could see her face, as smooth and untroubled and calm as ever; and admire her neat, long-nailed fingers curled on the scissors. 'Is that OK,' she said, 'or do you want more off?'

'That's great. Terrific. What do you think about

them, Tsu – our attackers, or invaders, or whatever they are?'

'I have stopped thinking about them.'

'Can you smell the smell?'

'I suppose so. If I want to. I don't want to.'

'What do you think it all means? Ispex says it's all tied up with The Pieces-of-Eight thing – the *Conqueror*, and the Octopus Emperor and all that –'

'The Octopus Emperor!' She gave a short, scornful laugh. 'You are all children, babies. With your fairy stories about Octopus Emperors and Pieces-of-Eight – '

'All the same, the *Conqueror* exploded. You don't deny that?'

'I don't deny it. I saw it. I didn't see any Octopus Emperors.'

'Then who blew up the *Conqueror*?'

She gave a slight shrug and said, 'Fizzy hair like yours is very difficult to cut. Mine is easy. I just bend forward and let it hang down and go snip-snip-snip. Then it is neat and tidy again. By the way, I won't be going aboard the ship from Epsilon Cool tomorrow. I am staying here.'

'Tsu! You can't do that! You're part of the whole thing. Everyone will be wanting to make a fuss of you!'

'Someone should stay here. You know I am right. The ship must not be left alone and un-guarded.'

'I thought you said you didn't believe in the attackers or whatever we seem to have with us!'

'I never said that. There is something strange happening. There is something new . . . something has entered the ship. I am not going to leave the ship unguarded. I will stay.'

'But, Tsu!'

'There, finished. You look quite nice now. I am staying here, on our ship, tomorrow.'

* * *

In the night Vawn awoke and began to scream. She stuffed a corner of her pillow into her mouth to hide the noise. The flies were over there, in the corner. A mass of them. They were circling round each other, a moving darkness in the darkness. If she reached out her arm, she could touch Tsu: but her arm was leaden, it would not move, she was afraid to move it. If she stretched it out, the dark cloud would whirr and settle on it and the smell of hot iron would suffocate her . . .

Staring-eyed, rigid with fear, she watched the slowly circling cloud. It was transparent, she could see through it, but it was real: a cloudy shape always changing shape, always moving, now nearer, now farther . . .

She bit the pillow. Tears from her staring eyes rolled down her cheeks. The cloud weaved and circled and spun. Then suddenly it rushed at her! – no, it swerved and curved away and the smell of hot metal brushed against her, carried on a chill current of air . . .

The cloud settled over Tsu's head and resumed its lazy circling.

The pale glimmer of a tiny neon, perpetually alight, gave just enough light for Vawn to see

Tsu's face. The cloud hovered above it. Tsu seemed to smile in her sleep.

Vawn's fear choked her. Somehow she escaped from her bed, blundered to the door and ran to the room shared by Makenzi and Ispex. 'I've seen them!' she gasped, shaking Makenzi awake. 'They're there! They're going to kill Tsu!'

Ispex groaned in his sleep. Makenzi, instantly awake, grabbed a Glo and swung out of his hammock. He and Vawn ran to Tsu. The light of the Glo showed nothing but Tsu's face. A slight smile touched the corner of her lips.

When Makenzi was back in his hammock, Vawn lay awake, clutching the covers with hands like claws. 'Mother!' she whispered. 'Tomorrow, Mother! I'll see you tomorrow!' But tomorrow seemed a black century away.

HOMECOMING

'There!' shouted Makenzi; and as he spoke, flung himself backwards from the real-vision window in an impossible somersault that landed him smack on his head, arms and legs everywhere. 'Yippee!' he shouted. 'Yippee! Glory hallelujah!' He rubbed his head and smiled until his face was all white teeth and ecstacy.

'It's even better here!' Ispex said, pushing his round head closer to the TV screen. On it, the shuttle ship from Epsilon Cool looked bigger than through the RV window: a purposeful, smooth, two-finned, sharklike shape, trailing double plumes of energy.

Only minutes ago, Vawn had seemed a ghost of herself with huge, shocked eyes. Now she changed. Her hair flew, her eyes became alive. 'Quick! Let me see!' She ran from the RV window to the TV screen and back again, her smiling mouth open as if she would eat the images of the ship from Epsilon Cool. 'In an hour from now . . . !' she said.

'Minutes from now!' Makenzi said. 'We're *rushing* at each other! How long in minutes, Shambles?'

'Six,' said Shambles.

'Six!' said Makenzi and tried to stand on his head. He kept falling over. 'Do it for me, Tsu!' he said. Obediently, she stood on her head while

Makenzi whooped and Ispex cheered her and Vawn stared at the RV. 'Bigger every moment!' she shouted. 'Come and see! Closer and closer! I can't believe it! Oh, Tsu, you must come with us and meet my mother and father and – '

Still balanced on her head and hands, Tsu calmly said, 'I told you. I'm staying here.'

Shambles said, 'I'm cutting all power. OK?'

'Yes, OK, OK, OK!' Makenzi cried. Now he was trying to do a handstand against a wall but the power cut affected the spin of the ship and its gravity. He fell sideways, laughing. 'How many minutes, Shambles?'

'Four.'

'Four, four, check the door!' sang Makenzi.

'Three, three, who do we see?' Vawn chanted.

'Two, two, whoopity-whoo!' Ispex sang, out of tune. Although he had remained still while the others were doing their crazy things, his face was scarlet with excitement. 'I'm going to check the hatch latch again,' he said, solemnly. At the door, he turned. '*Hatch latch*,' he said. 'That's quite funny.' Suddenly his solemn face beamed.

'Just look at that shuttle!' Makenzi said, hugging himself. 'Screaming along! Filling the whole screen now! Ecosuits on, everyone – '

'But I don't want to wear my suit, you can't *feel* people through ecosuits!' Vawn said.

'Take 'em off if the docking goes OK – and it will,' said Makenzi, 'but put it on for now, just in case. OK?'

Starstormer began to vibrate. 'What was that?' Vawn said, her face suddenly frightened. 'Our parents, you idiot!' Makenzi said. 'Shock waves from their ship! Don't look like that, we're nearly there! They'll go right round us to slew off power, and then bring in their blasters and then – '

'And then!' Vawn said. 'Oh yes, and *then* . . . '

'One minute,' said Shambles. 'Fifty seconds . . . Forty seconds . . . '

Tsu sniffed. She could smell hot iron.

She smiled.

* * *

The big, sharklike shuttle ship spat flame, curtsied and began to sideslip, tail out. More flame. She almost spun on herself. Had she been a car, her back tyres would have screamed. But she was a spaceshuttle, a craft of infinite power and controllability; and guiding her was Makenzi's father Jass, a man who would have made a great racing driver in the old days. He smiled and touched a button.

The ship jetted burning gas and slewed into a still tighter turn – so tight that his wife, Verona, was thrown against his shoulder. He put his arm round her and held her. Her smile was as radiant as his. 'That . . . *thing*,' she said, wonderingly, staring out at the meteorite cockleshell that seemed to be curving past the window. 'They've been in space, for I don't know how long, in that thing . . . ' She shuddered.

'I know,' he replied. 'But it's all over now. They're almost with us. And soon we'll all be together, on Epsilon Cool, whether the settlement's ready or no.'

'Ready or no,' she said; and reached up to kiss his cheek.

The ship began to feel jelly-like as Jass played thrust against thrust. 'That does it,' he murmured. 'A little more . . . so . . . And another little more . . . Then – *cut.*'

He flicked his fingers over a row of buttons. Lights went out. There was a very slight bump. 'Nice,' he said. 'Lovely. That bump was our son knocking on the door, Verona. And your daughter, Sheila.'

'And our son,' said Meg, Ispex's mother. She stood in the doorway of the control chamber, her hand in her husband's. Her plump face was alight and glorious.

There was a grumbling sound and a loudspeaker voice said, 'Locked and docked. Docked OK.' Then, 'Atmos equalised. Equalised OK.' Then, 'Our port open OK, they seem to have some difficulty opening theirs – No, they don't, their port's open OK, here they come, our visitors . . . '

The loudspeaker voice spoke to an empty room. The people were gone: gone to spread their arms wide, then encircle and hug and hold the smaller figures that, one by one, stumbled towards them, blinded and choked with happiness.

Alone on Starstormer, *Tsu waited. She sat still and silent, her hands folded on her lap, her eyes calm and unfocussed.*

Suddenly Shambles broke the silence. 'Attack!' he shouted, 'Attack, attack! We are being attacked!'

'Be quiet, Shambles. I know.'

'But the flies! – the attackers! – they are close, they are everywhere!'

'Be quiet.'

'But there is danger, danger, danger, danger!'

Tsu leaned forward and cancelled Shambles. The machine became silent.

In the small, grey-black room in which Tsu waited, there appeared a shimmering. A sheen of gold. A glassy, luminous sheen, filled with – what were they? – motes of dust, whirling flies? The shimmering strengthened. Tsu smiled, very faintly. Her finger traced the Sign of Eight over her breast. Her nostrils widened. Hot iron.

The shimmering hardened into glassy golden planes: and the Captain of Conqueror *was there, smiling. 'You did well, Tsu,' he said.*

At Tsu's feet, Shambles somehow defeated his cancelled status. 'Danger!' he croaked. 'The enemy! The enemy is here! Danger!'

'Cancel that thing,' smiled the Captain. Without looking down, Tsu prodded at Shambles with her toe.

Shambles' lights died. His voice croaked into silence. The Captain smiled.

'Nine of them!' said the Captain. 'How well you have done, Tsu! Nine! Three remarkable children; and their parents, six highly trained adults. Nine perfect specimens delivered into our hands!'

'Hands?' said Tsu.

The Captain laughed almost boyishly. 'Well, not exactly our "hands",' he said. 'But that is our problem, isn't it? Not having hands. Not having bodies, legs, arms. Not having fingers and muscles to use tools. Only our minds, Tsu. Only that great central mind, in charge of a world of dust . . . dust haunting the universe, everlastingly driven to invasion and conquest in search of –'

'I've brought you nine bodies,' Tsu said. 'Good bodies, the best. Now you can occupy them. And now you must give me my reward, please!'

The Captain did not answer her. 'Look, Tsu!' he said, pointing at the TV screen. 'We're closing in! Look! See how the screen darkens as our world wraps itself round these two little ships! Aboard that other ship, that shuttle, no doubt your friends are still kissing each other, hugging each other . . . Well, they have lips and arms, they are humans . . . But look, Tsu! Our world is winning the true victory!'

Tsu looked at the TV screen. The shuttle was still visible, but the dark cloud was enveloping it, shadowing it, devouring it: like millions of black flies. That was what Vawn had thought them. She looked away. 'My parents,' she said. 'You promised. You have had my parents nearly all my life. Now I want them back, I want them for myself. You promised.'

'Now the screen is black,' said the Captain. 'Now we,

they, all of us, are locked in my world. All thanks to you, Tsu. I wonder which of the new bodies I myself shall inhabit?'

'My parents,' said Tsu. 'Take me to them! Let me see them! I did what you told me to do!'

'Of course, of course!' said the Captain. His smile was wide and radiant. 'Happiness, Tsu: you've earned it! Come to me, dear child. That's right, come to me! Don't mind the glass, that is not real, there is no barrier between us . . .'

He spread his arms wide in welcome. Slowly, Tsu rose to her feet. She drew a deep breath, raised her arms in front of her as if to part curtains, took a short, careful step – then another –

The shimmering glass enfolded her, lighting her small, tense body with gold.

And then she was beyond the glass and the Captain's arms were spread wide. He was walking backwards, welcoming arms outspread, backwards and backwards, always smiling, backwards down an endless vista of shimmering glass; and she followed as if sleepwalking, her arms raised to him, her curved fingers arched upwards, quivering.

'Give me my parents,' she murmured from her half sleep. Flies buzzed drowsily in her brain.

'Of course, of course!' smiled the Captain. 'Just follow me! Of course, of course, of course!'

END

More adventures of the Starstormers in

SUNBURST

The second story in the
Starstormer Saga

THE AWAKENING WATER

G. R. Kesteven

When the strange girl told John that the duty-men doped all the children's water to keep them quiet he did not believe her. After all, she was only one of the 'Lost Ones', one of those who had run away from the Party's protection to live in the wilds. It wasn't until John tasted pure water – the Awakening Water – again that he realised the true implication of what she had said and suddenly knew that he too must escape.

THE PALE INVADERS

G. R. Kesteven

Life was peaceful in the secluded valley where Gerald and Susan lived with the others. No danger threatened them. They did not know what had happened so long ago. But one day Gerald found out. What he discovered made him very scared indeed. And then the pale strangers appeared in the valley, bringing with them the dark shadow of the past.